# DRESSAGE
## FOR THE
# NEW AGE

Dominique Barbier
with Mary Daniels

SIMON & SCHUSTER
NEW YORK  LONDON  TORONTO  SYDNEY  TOKYO  SINGAPORE

**FIRESIDE**
Simon & Schuster Building
Rockefeller Center
1230 Avenue of the Americas
New York, New York 10020

First Fireside Edition 1993
FIRESIDE and colophon are registered trademarks of
Simon & Schuster Inc.
Designed by Richard Oriolo
Line art by Candy Cohen
Manufactured in the United States of America


3   5   7   9   10   8   6   4


Library of Congress Cataloging in Publication Data

Barbier, Dominique, date.
Dressage for the new age/by Dominique Barbier with
Mary Daniels.
p    cm.
Includes index.
1. Dressage.   2. New Age movement.   I. Daniels, Mary,
date.   II. Title.
SF309.5B36 1990
798.2'3—dc20                                    89-8850   CIP
ISBN 0-671-76269-9

*To Debra, Domina, and Tianna,
and to all the horses that shared
their lives with me.*
—DOMINIQUE BARBIER

*To the memory of Roxana Daniels,
who loved horses, 1963–1988.*
—MARY DANIELS

# CONTENTS

Contents

## Part III

## THE MOVEMENTS

# FOREWORD

Many books have been published in this country on the subject of the training of the horse, or dressage. Unfortunately for the trainer who is interested in learning, almost all of these books have been written by research people or people who are writers, not riders or trainers. Sydney Felton, in his good book *Masters of Equitation,* said that more than 90 percent of books on training are written by research people. The author of this book, Dominique Barbier, is one of the great trainers. He knows his subject from a lifetime of training horses and people. He is one of the few authors who deals with the subject of lightness in the horse, and he does it as no one else has ever done it.

Perhaps equally as important is the manner in which this book is written. While Barbier offers much as a talented horseman, Mary Daniels has made this a most entertaining read. Of all the books I have read on this subject, few have been as easy for a horseman to understand as this one—principally because it was put together by a famous writer and, just as important, a horsewoman with years of experience working with professionals at riding and training her own horses.

Every horseman interested in training would do well to read and study this book.

—CHUCK GRANT

# INTRODUCTION

Given the large number of theoretical books already available to students of dressage, why would I seek to add yet another to those already written? Because through my riding, training, teaching, studying, and observing, I have developed what I believe is a substantially different approach. It is one that I have sought, through my teaching, to organize and systematize, in order to be able to explain it accurately to a wide audience. My goal was not to write just another book on riding, but to give a fresh outlook on a centuries-old art.

I feel those who have written about training horses over the last hundred years have been involved in methods and rationales that have little to do with real life and real horses. They have been preoccupied with writing prescriptions. My own philosophy of riding is closely allied to my personal philosophy of life. I believe that the two are irrevocably related. People ride the way they are, mentally, emotionally, spiritually. That is why horses perform differently for different riders.

For centuries the human intellect has been held in the highest esteem, while anything relating to the body was placed at the bottom of the ladder. This idea has grown to the point that man has actually lost a realistic contact with his own nature. Society has succeeded in alienating and bastardizing his sensibilities in order to control him, to the point where man is now required to relearn everything—how to eat a balanced diet, how to make love, how to feel his feet on the earth, and even how to feel good and relaxed in his own skin and make another human being feel good. I feel man today is looking for something different, trying to rediscover his natural senses, awareness, and abilities.

I believe strongly in the New Age in which we are living. It is bringing about a revolutionary change in the way we think about life as well as a new awareness and expression of the way we understand the world around us. The key to this change is the development of a realization of the limitlessness of consciousness, and the possibility of enlightenment. We are beginning to see a convergence between ancient and modern ideas and between Eastern and Western philosophies that leads in these directions. There is also a convergence between science and spirituality, and a rediscovery of the sacred, a revitalization of the dialogue between the human and the divine.

Zen philosophy tells us that every point is the center of the universe. We are living in a time of discovery of that insight in every field of human understanding, from psychology to ecology to health care. I believe we must also find a way to a more humane, ethical, and spiritual treatment of and relationship with the animals with whom we share the earth. We see this already in the rising opposition to the exploitation of wild animals. As this evolves, we will see a revolutionary change in the way we act toward domesticated animals, such as horses, as well.

Although my method derives in large part from my heritage in the French classical school of equitation, my training in England and Portugal, in addition to my extensive work with American horses and riders, has led me in new directions. For example, one of the reasons I wrote this book is to reexplain the nearly lost goal of mental harmony between horse and rider to a wider audience than I can reach by my teaching. Too many people treat the horse as though he were a machine, without ever realizing the fantastic world that is his mind. Some people actually enjoy a mechanical horse that has no spirit, soul, or life. These people, whether they realize it or not, are looking for a mechanical system of training and riding a horse. This, of course, produces a mechanical result.

The French method of riding and training horses, based on lightness, provides the philosophy in which my method is rooted. This philosophy is neither widely understood nor actualized in modern dressage. However, it is alive in the minds and hearts of many sensitive and open-minded people.

Already, I believe, there are many riders who are frustrated with the push-and-pull method, one that is as difficult for both horse and rider as is an argumentative relationship between two human beings. These riders want something simpler, more adapted to a new way of thinking. They are attracted to my approach, which is different because I believe an open mind is needed to relate to and mentally understand the horse. This approach emphasizes listening to and following the constantly flowing dialogue between horse and rider. This is, however, an approach that baffles many other people and even frightens some. They look at me without comprehension when I teach. Yet what I attempt to do is something very basic, fundamental, and natural, that can be mastered without the use of force.

Most teachers of riding try to outline only the physical concepts. Very few, to my knowledge, ever mention or teach that the most important aid in riding is the mind. I believe 90 percent of riding is mental, allowing the horse to move and perform for and of himself. The horse will accept some firm actions if they are done for him and not against him, with no anger and with a calm and cool mind. However, most of my emphasis is on a brain-to-brain communication between a rider and his horse.

More specifically, riding should consist of asking the horse politely for what you wish. No kicking, pushing, driving, spurring, or whipping. Think first, then ask your horse for what you want. You will be surprised at how good the results are. Visualization, the power of the mind, is the most important aid. Think and the horse will respond.

Here is a very simple exercise to demonstrate this concept: To make any horse turn to the right, make sure you have a reasonably forward-going horse in a *controlled* walk. Have both lower legs softly in contact with the horse's sides. Look to the right and think about going there. The horse will turn to the right. Thinking and determination come before anything else. One should be able to communicate with a horse by mental visualization, brain to brain, in the very simplest movements, such as turning in a certain direction, as well as in exercises of extreme collection, such as *piaffer* and *passage*.

In the art of riding, the only physical part for the horse is a number of suppling exercises meant to make him fit and a better athlete. If your goal is suppleness, these exercises must be done in complete relaxation, mental and physical, of both horse and rider. If you force, you contract the horse. You actually make him worse, not better, because you create mental and physical stress.

Riding itself is not difficult. Using the mind, however, can be difficult if you are not accustomed to applying it as an aid in riding. Nor can you train without love. This will sound airy, perhaps, but only deep love and understanding coordinated with refined tact will give you positive results with horses.

My method may be different, but it is a better one because it is easier, especially for the horse, and I believe many people will enjoy using it. It is actually the oldest way of riding.

Rares sont les cavaliers qui, veritablement passiones par le cheval et son dressage, s'interessent profondement à ce dressage, avec abnégation, et font de ce travail, extraordinairement subtil, une des préoccupations dominantes de leur vie.

Rare is the rider who is truly passionate about the horse and his training, taking a profound interest in dressage with self-abnegation, and making this extraordinarily subtle work one of the dominant motivations in his life.

—NUNO OLIVEIRA
*Reflections on Equestrian Art*

## Part I

# THE PART OF RIDING NO ONE TALKS ABOUT

# The Experiences
# That Changed My
# Attitude

A simple and interesting way to explain my approach is to go back and find its sources.

By the time I was fourteen years old, I already had an understanding of the importance of mood in riding, of emotions and their consequences on the rider's physiological and mental states. I had started riding when I was twelve or thirteen, in Poitiers, France, at the Jesuit school, where part of the curriculum was riding. We did a little jumping and a little basic dressage. I loved it and wanted more.

I did well. There are easy horses and there are difficult horses; I always got the bad guys. I thought of it as a good sign.

I worked with teachers who had military backgrounds. In their thinking there was no room for the way the rider or the horse felt. Some days I felt it would be better to start work with the walk, other times with the trot. But I had to conform to a very rigid way of thinking, which said work *always* began the same way. I began to feel that this approach was wrong. I realized that what my instructors were teaching me were mechanical, physical things. When I asked questions about anything beyond that, I was given no answer.

At fourteen I moved to a stable owned by a man who imported Irish horses and Connemara ponies, where more formal instruction was available. I had an instructor—a graduate of Saumur, the French military school—who gave me lessons for which I paid. On a regular basis, the owner would put me on big horses that had never been ridden before, leave, and close the doors to the arena. He would come back twenty minutes later. If I was still on the horse, well and good. If not, a torrent of invective was rained on me. One time—it was the middle of winter—the horse I was on jumped a six-foot-high door and landed outdoors on the ice. It was an effective if unconventional way to begin to develop a good seat and to get a lot of experience. I did this sort of thing, on and off, for three years.

When I was fifteen I went to Crabbett Park, a school for young riders, in England. I observed the class that instructors took to become a Fellow of the British Horse Society, the highest course in dressage in England, and I asked to ride in that class. My teacher, Brian Young, FBHS (Fellowship of the British Horse Society), agreed, thinking, I imagine, "I will put him in the back. He won't understand much, because he doesn't speak English."

There were six students, with me at the end of the line on a bad horse. Every time the teacher asked me to do something, I did it. At the end of the course, the administrator talked to my father in English, which I translated into French. He asked if I could return to carry on with a professional course. When I was seventeen-and-a-half years old, I completed the normal three-month British Horse Society Assistant Instructor (BHSAI) course in two months. I then went back to France, where I raced trotters, steeplechased, and did flat racing. I also managed the stables at a government agricultural college close to the Swiss border.

I returned to England in 1972, when I was twenty-two, to the Talland School of Equitation in Cirenchester. There, thanks to a beautiful thoroughbred mare, Golden Caledon, I started to develop a feeling for an approach different from the one to which I had previously been exposed.

At the time I was completely misdirected in my goals. I wanted to be as good a rider, technically, as I could be. I developed a series of tricks in order to be able to ride and train horses better and more quickly (I thought), but the results were only temporary. When a problem reappeared, I had to redo my trick over and over again. The tricks had very little educational value for the horse, but I was very certain about their value and very strong in their application.

Mine was an acrobatic approach. I had a lot of shortcuts. I used to put my horses in a very fixed, rigid frame, and I didn't want them to deviate from it. I was very successful with this approach in jumping.

Then Golden Caledon was given to me to ride. She was very beautiful and very refined. During the first fifteen days I tried to ride her, it was a disaster. I was unable to walk the horse, trot her, or do anything at my will. She made me realize over and over again how useless my physical-trick approach really was. Since I was young and ambitious, this lesson was hard to accept.

For those fifteen rainy spring days, as I tried to ride Golden Caledon through the beautiful English fields, her mind was on what was behind every hedge, on the seagulls in the next field, or on something she imagined looked like a hound hunting a fox. There was no communication between us. Nor could I take physical hold of her. I used all my physical tricks to restrain and restrict her, day after day, but nothing worked. She just did not care, and ignored me. She did her own thing when she wanted to do it. Her mind was on everything, everywhere, but not with me.

At the end of what seemed like an interminable period, my instructor (and the owner of Golden Caledon), Mrs. Molly Siveright, FBHS, DBHS (Donor British Horse Society), who I was sure had been observing every failure of mine, asked me if I wanted some help. I did. When you are cooking in your own juice for fifteen days, you are ready to try anything. If she had said, "Sit on your head," I would have done it. I wanted another trick, a better one than those I knew. All my old ones didn't work. But Mrs. Siveright simply told me, "Walk around the field and listen to the birds."

Listen to the birds! The field seemed so large to me, listening to those birds. Mrs. Siveright made sure I walked the mare around it twice. The immediate result was that the mare's walk was much calmer than before.

It's not that I did something mechanical. There's a way of calming your intellectual mind and letting your animal mind come up so you can just be one with the horse. As soon as your mind relaxes, your body relaxes; the horse senses the mood through your body and reacts to it. It can go in either direction; just as a horse reacts to stress, he reacts to relaxation.

Reading my mind again, my instructor asked me if I wanted to try something else now. Impatiently I waited for what I thought would be the secret. What she said was, "For whatever you want, just ask politely."

Now I was even more angry. But Mrs. Siveright left me on my own to listen to the birds and to be polite. It seemed laughable. But when I politely asked the mare to trot, we went happily around the field! In a week we were the best of friends. When we got together, it was wonderful. As little communication as we had had before, we had an abundance of it now.

That experience proved to be an important revelation in clarifying my attitude toward horses as well as toward life in general. Riding was not a series of tricks but a relationship with the horse based on friendship, trust, and mutual respect.

A second experience impressed upon me how deep, in fact, that relationship could be, and the new world it could open to me. When I started flying changes with Golden Caledon, they came calmly, with no problems. Then, the more I asked, the more she came to anticipate, and not just in the location of the change. It was not just a matter of routine; as soon as the thought "flying change" came into my head, she did it.

I was amazed! Could a horse read a person's mind so well?

I realized I was thinking too loudly and decided that I had to develop another way of thinking. I knew what I was doing was a positive thing, but I had to organize its use.

That was when I started to develop the ability to create two minds: one that was readily available to the horse, that he could read, and another, far removed behind the first, whose information was not available to him.

The first would say, "I am going to do nothing," while the second would whisper, "I am going to do a flying change over there by the big bush." My new technique amazed me by its instant and constant success in eliminating the possibility of what people call "anticipation" but in reality is the horse's ability to read your mind more quickly than you can imagine.

For the next eight years I continued my search for better communication and understanding with my horses, using visualization with the power of the mind as the most important aid. I found that the true art of riding is having the complicity of your horse before you start working him.

My goals changed. When I was in England my objective had been to have a degree, a piece of paper to show my father that I had graduated from a school.

When I was in France and England, riding consisted entirely of jumping and three-day events. But I knew the solution to success in both was dressage. I decided that if I wanted to continue to learn, dressage had to be the first priority, the finest thing I could study.

I tried to apply to Saumur, but I learned I would have to join the French Army for seven years, and I didn't want to do that.

Then I went to Portugal and I found what I was looking for when I saw Mestre Nuno Oliveira ride. My goal was now to study with him. I thought, This man is able to do things no one else can. I had to ask why. What Mestre Nuno Oliveira did for me was to confirm the things that I already felt about riding. "That's good, carry on," he would say, when I would do something that got results.

One of the most powerful experiences that changed my

whole concept about riding happened in the very beginning of my stay at the Mestre's. I hardly knew him then. I would watch him ride at five o'clock every morning. He used to ride a big gray horse that had had an accident, and as a result had a displacement of the hips. The Mestre was the only one who rode him.

One morning he asked me, out of the blue, to come down out of the gallery to the ring and ride the gray horse. He asked me to canter in a circle and then he said, *"Descente de main et descente de jambe."*

I knew how to do that, that it meant no action with the hands or legs—complete passivity. Then he asked me to drop the rein to the buckle. I did. Next, he asked me to lengthen the stride at the canter down the long side and go into a big circle. That was no problem. I loosened my back and the horse went into a long frame and extended.

Then he told me to collect the horse, and of course my first reaction was to take back the contact with the reins. The Mestre just said, "No!"

Therefore, I had to *think* how to collect my horse from an extended canter without reins. I put my body into a collected attitude, stretching upward and bringing my shoulders back; and that very large horse came back to a perfect collected canter, the reins still at the buckle.

That brief experience changed my whole thinking about riding, and I knew that if I could do just one thing with a horse, this was what I wanted it to be.

Now I am trying to put into words these things about riding that so far have been left unsaid.

Another important experience that confirmed my beliefs while I was studying with the Mestre in Portugal was my work with the Lusitanian stallion Dom Giovanni. I loved Dom Giovanni from the moment I saw him, long before I was allowed to purchase him. His owner, Senhor Engineer Fernando Sommer D'Andrade, the son of Dom Guy D'Andrade, is a Federation Equestre International (FEI) judge, and comes from a family that has more than four hundred years of experience in breeding Lusitano horses.

I wanted another horse after I had bought my first one, Dom Pasquale, from Senhor Pala, a breeder near Villa Franca, so I had gone to see Senhor Andrade. He showed me some young stallions, all beautiful, and all beyond my financial possibilities. Walking through the stables, I found Giovanni, tied down with a thick chain that cut deep into his neck. I asked about the horse and learned that he had crippled a groom by striking the man's shoulder. Considered dangerous, Giovanni was not for sale. In fact, at the age of four, he was going to be destroyed. The Andrade horses are noted for their impeccable dispositions, and the breeder was not ready to jeopardize his reputation by selling such an animal.

Hesitantly, I asked if I could see Giovanni move. Although his conformation impressed me, especially his beautiful neck and shoulder, he was the worst mover I had ever seen. I believed he had a mental block that would not allow his body to move, and I thought that I could work with him.

I told the breeder so. "No," he told me. "The only way you could have the horse is if the Mestre would approve."

The Mestre said no. So I replied, "All right, but go and get him for yourself because he is a fantastic horse."

Eventually the Mestre said yes, and I didn't wait long when he did. "I'm going right now," I replied.

I told the breeder I would take the horse for a month and pay all the expenses. "If I can't walk, trot, and canter him within a month, you can destroy him. If I can ride him after that time, he's mine," I said.

This particular breeder, Senhor Andrade, has some of the coldest-blooded horses in all of Portugal, but once in a while a horse is born that gets all the fire that should have gone into the rest. It took four people to hold Giovanni the first time I got on him. He was a very high-strung, hypersensitive horse, afraid of everything. He could not take work that was done halfway correctly. I had to be absolutely correct with him. Because of this uncompromising situation, I had to do everything mentally and as little as possible physically.

For three weeks Giovanni stayed facing the wall because he

was impossible to control when he was straight. Then we did a lot of stopping and stretching down at the halt, which was one of the most difficult things for him to do as he was so contracted. Then we would take two or three steps, then stop again and stretch down again. That was mentally very demanding for this horse, because he wanted to *go*. He didn't want to stop and think. That exercise also served to put us together mentally. He finally began to relax. I started the *passage* first, before the trot, because the *passage* was the only gait in which he could relax. When he relaxed at the *passage*, I went to the trot and tried to maintain his relaxation.

Then Giovanni was injured trying to kick another horse. I had to give him seven injections a day, and it was an acrobatic performance to get a needle into him. He would contract the muscles in his neck and the needle would come flying out. After a few days, however, he realized I was helping him, and he had a change of mind.

A month later, after a lot of sweat, and thanks to the Mestre, who started me off on the right foot with him, Giovanni made it. But he required an enormous amount of constant love, understanding, and patience. Since then, Giovanni has been my most brilliant horse as far as his mental ability and his general nature go. He has become a real companion. He has learned tempi changes, *passage, piaffer,* Spanish walk and trot, canter pirouettes in series, canter on the spot, and the canter backward.

Allow me to relate a recent experience showing the camaraderie and close communication we have developed. One day I was helping my assistant perform *passage* on my other stallion, Dom Pasquale. She was experiencing difficulty with this movement. I was very intensely involved with her work, visualizing *passage*, while sitting on Giovanni, who was on a loose rein. Suddenly he began to *passage* for me! I was amazed, since I knew that this horse normally needed considerable readjustment of his balance and position before attempting this movement. Technically speaking, what he was doing was impossible, but he was doing it nevertheless! What an impression that made on me, concerning the power of mental communication with the horse!

It was the best illustration of visualization possible. Physically, I wasn't doing anything. If you want it badly enough, the horse does it. As a footnote, I want to say that in this book I express my belief that very little that is physical is needed to ride a horse. When I long-rein a horse, I have proof of my belief, because although there is nobody on the horse, the horse performs. Of course, in the beginning there *is* a physical part, but it is only a reinforcement of the mind. Progressively, it becomes less and less necessary, and ultimately, is not necessary at all. I know what some people want me to say: that when I think of doing a movement I move my body just enough to cause the horse to react. That's *not* what I am saying. The more you develop the mind, the less you need the body. I am applying the principle of "less is more" to the art of riding.

Recently a fifteen-year-old girl rode my stallions for a week. I was surprised because I had only little details to correct in her. She offered the horses a clear picture of what she wanted. It is when people become older that their brains get clouded by complications in life—troubles with their parents or with their boyfriends—and when they ride, the horse reacts in a way that mirrors those problems. Kids can do whatever they want to on a horse so easily because they don't have any preconceptions in their minds.

Another chapter in my self-education opened when I first came to the United States in the mid-1970s. I taught in clinic situations, where I was given very little time with an individual horse, so I had to establish communication with him very quickly.

Most problems I came across were with spoiled or abused horses. In those cases, I often had to dominate the horse in order to induce it to trust man again, to break through the defensive barriers the animals had usually erected to protect themselves. (My definition of domination is making sure the animal is willing to share with you.) In such situations I had to attempt to make a fast estimate of which defenses were mental and which were physical.

For instance, one horse might associate some movement or position with discomfort. He might have a mental flashback to a situation that had been frightening or demeaning to him. It is very difficult for a horse to overcome fear. If a horse has a bad leg and fear in his brain, he is going to be difficult to convince there is a better life. His brain is saying, "You are in big trouble, protect yourself!"

In order to establish myself quickly and successfully in a working communication with these horses, my own mental attitude proved crucial. An open, analytical, unconditionally accepting attitude is necessary, with no room for anger or a sense of superiority.

It helped me in the beginning to analyze what we have made of the horse. He is a living being that is locked in a jail cell, his stall, for twenty-three hours a day. Then the rider takes the horse out and gives the horse whatever emotions he feels, whether or not the rider is conscious of it. Even if it is just a matter of dark or bright, depressed or optimistic, an unconscious visualization of the rider's emotions is projected onto the horse.

I found that I could create an instant relationship and communication with the horse if I could get rid of all the negative, preconceived ideas I might have. Once I could accomplish this, I found I could shorten the amount of time establishing a relationship took. What is involved is this: when you sit on the horse, you tell him very clearly, "I want *this*. And I don't want *that*." This, again, is visualization. You tell your horse what frame you want him in. You have a very clear idea of what you want to achieve, and you keep flashing mental pictures of it to him.

Very often, riders concentrate on the forty-nine problems they have while they ride, and they don't care if they have a relationship with the horse, or if he really knows what they want him to do. An anecdote illustrates what I mean. Once I was giving a clinic in the East. In it was a lady on her Appaloosa. He walked too fast on a long rein. I asked her once, I asked her twice, then three times, to shorten the rein and put her horse together and start to have a slow and "together" walk with the horse on the bit. And nothing ever happened. She made no attempt. The rein was at the buckle.

"Dominique," she told me, "I read in a horse magazine that

Appaloosas have an eye disease that makes them stumble and unfit to have a proper walk, and sometimes it even makes them pace." She added that the veterinarian was coming out later to say for sure if her horse had this disease, but she already believed that it did.

I did not understand what all this eye business was about, so, first of all, I ignored it. I just went through the basic technique I use when I want to put together two minds that are not communicating with one another. I tell the rider to walk six strides and halt. Then walk another six strides and halt. And walk six more strides and halt. The two brains are put together that way. Each time the rider halts his horse, he does a little less. You can stop the physical business after a while, and thus you make the mental communication the more important part.

In the case of the Appaloosa, after three or four minutes the horse was stopping and walking like a normal animal. In fact, horse and rider started to "dance" together and accepted the rules of the dance. (A friend who had been watching all this on the side said to me, "Dominique, that was the quickest eye surgery I ever saw.")

I often see something similar happen with riders who seem to be physically limited, but who do better once their mental communication with the horse improves. If you are like most riders, reasonably fit, consider the possibilities of how much better you can become by improving your mental communication with your horse. Work on your ability to make your mind ask things clearly of him. Visualize.

# 2

# *The Power of the Mind as the Most Important Aid*

A variety of books has been written on the nonphysical improvement of skills in sports, such as *The Inner Game of Skiing* and *The Inner Game of Tennis*. My goal is to open your mind to a similar approach in riding, which allows the rider to obtain more by doing less.

Most of my emphasis is on mental communication between the rider and his horse. In this approach, using the power of the mind in the form of visualization is the most important aid. The rider is simply asked to prepare the horse, building impulsion, positioning him correctly for certain movements. Then he has but to think, and the horse will understand and respond.

Remember the simple exercise we gave in the introduction? To make a horse turn to the right, prepare him, think about going to the right, and he will. Carry this into other exercises and you will soon realize that riding is not difficult, but using thinking as an aid to riding can be hard if you are not used to doing it.

Today, as in centuries past, there are those who have tried to mystify the world of horses and the art of riding. They have made knowledge a mystery. But the only magic about it is that there *is* no secret. Horses are a part of life the same way that any other relationship is a part of life.

The worst fault I find with the typical rider is that he is not clear in his mind about what he wants from the horse, and the horse then becomes confused. It is very important for the rider or trainer to think about what he wants from the horse. Always ask with the mind first, and then with the body. You should know where you are going and then take the necessary steps to get there. The horse cannot possibly perform correctly if the rider doesn't have a clear picture of the movement to be performed.

Visualization is similar to you and your horse watching television. Visualization is the rider bombarding the screen with pictures—clearer ones every time. If you are not transmitting or sending the pictures that appear on the TV screen, and the horse is putting them there, you are in big trouble. If the screen is blank to begin with, the horse is going to fill it up by sending his own pictures. If the horse shies, it means the TV screen was blank, and he replaced the picture of you trotting calmly in a big circle with a picture of a snake in the corner. (If the horse won't watch the television screen, tap him with the whip.)

Already there is evidence that humans can communicate with animals such as dolphins through visualization. A magazine article tells the story of an Australian man who has an incredible relationship with a dolphin friend. Every time the Australian takes his fishing boat out to sea, the dolphin comes with him. When the fisherman wants to come home, he visualizes the harbor, and the dolphin turns around and heads home before the man can begin to turn the boat. The same article tells about a boy who sends his dolphin friend out to retrieve a certain kind of seaweed for him. There are three or four kinds in the area; he sends the dolphin a mental picture of the one that he wants, and the latter never fails to bring that particular variety back.

The first and foremost step for my type of training is for the rider to establish a mental relationship with his horse. The horse must know what the rider expects, and the rider must be confident he will receive the horse's cooperation without force. Calm determination should be the rider's credo. It is up to the human partner to "listen to" and understand the horse's mental and physical problems, and then to ease them.

It is not only with your eyes and ears that you are going to "listen." You must try to have a clever seat, one that has its own sensory intake that feels the mechanism of the horse's gaits and its peculiarities. You must educate your seat to feel the movement of the horse's back, his difficulties, his relative suppleness, and his roundness.

Your legs must likewise have their own sensory intake. Try to feel your horse breathing through your lower leg. Then try to breathe in unison with your horse, something that is very important, especially for the work in hand, because it encourages animal communication between the two of you. I confess I don't know how breathing together works. Every time people are conscious of their breathing, they relax. Perhaps breathing together is part of what leads to relaxation. I only know it is similar to what happens when two strange dogs meet; they try to breathe in unison. If they can, they don't fight. If they can't, they do fight.

My method requires a combination of acute mental awareness along with a lot of relaxation in the body. Tension of any sort will disturb the horse-and-rider pair. (This is the problem that comes from using the driving leg and the restraining hand.)

▬▬▬

Ultimately, you ride a horse the way you are, mentally and culturally, and the various schools of riding that exist today are the expression of the culture, and a reflection of the national character, of the country where the type of riding was developed. For example, certain cultures developed forms of riding, such as foxhunting and cross-country riding, that are done primarily outdoors.

If you hunt your horse with a "dead" body on it for two years, the horse is going to learn to take care of itself in difficult situations. Such riders expect their horses to discover collection for themselves. However, collection does not come by itself with the passing of time. If you trot for three hours a day in the wrong position, you will not discover collection any more than you would learn classical dance by crawling around on your hands and knees for the same amount of time.

My background, as I have said, is in the French classical school, which looks upon dressage as an *art de vivre*—a living, performing art, similar to ballet. My method is applicable to all types of riding, but especially to dressage.

It seems to me that the great *ecuyers,* or riding masters of the past—François Robichon de la Gueriniere (1688–1751), François Baucher (1796–1873), and others—were all looking for the same thing: *"descente de main et descente de jambe."* This French expression means "the relaxing of the hands and the legs"; in other words, a cessation of action.

Baucher expressed it another way: "Make yourself understood and let it happen." This achievement resembles a state of grace, of ultimate perfection, because it lets the horse move and perform on his own, from within himself. The horse cannot understand this refinement of aids that makes use of only slight leg pressure and no hands, unless the mental relationship, the mental harmony between rider and horse, has first been established.

Man is supposed to be the most perfect animal because he thinks. However, communicating mentally with horses is actually far easier than doing so with other humans, because the latter have learned to use many faces, to play many roles. In other words, people cheat. We all learn at a very early age that it's appropriate to say certain things and use certain smiles in certain situations. Horses don't do this. Once we allow the horse to reveal his own personality, he remains basically the same.

Also, many of us have a bad habit of not putting things into the proper words. We use words to a disadvantage, because quite frequently talking actually disturbs true communication instead of enhancing it.

Each of us has had the experience of living for a number of years with a person with whom, after a while, words are not necessary. We can actually sense his or her thoughts and interpret them without verbal interaction. How many times has a friend opened his mouth to say something, and you already know what he's about to tell you? There's nothing strange about this. It's natural and should be used to advantage with horses. It works even better with them because you don't have words, language, to interfere.

As I mentioned before, most of the time when I am with a student, I do not teach riding. I find I first have to reconnect people to feel their own bodies. What they finally learn often turns out to be not only applicable to riding but to all of life.

I do believe, after a number of years of practicing and teaching mental communication between horse and rider, both at the lower and higher levels of dressage, that horses have different levels of intelligence just as people do. They also have more or less awareness, and are more or less willing to use it, just like people. Some like their work immensely, some are great personalities, and some make great friends. They all have something to teach us.

I also believe that horses are the closest to God in the animal world. Horses are karmic and they come to us in our lives karmically, when it is time for us truly to learn. We must not miss this occasion to learn, as it will enrich other areas of our lives. When you are frustrated in this learning process, do not become angry at your horse. Remember the old Arab proverb that says, "Your horse is your mirror." Learn what your horse has to teach you, then apply it to something else in your life.

# 3

## *Search for Excellence, Discovery of Perfection*

M any people will believe that they will have problems visualizing, that it is difficult to do. Which technique you use is not as important as what you visualize. If you go around the ring on a horse, or in life, seeing yourself as a failure in your mind, that is what you will become in reality.

Most trainers, riders, and judges could have a clearer idea in their minds of what picture they want from the combination of horse and rider. They may know what they like when they see it, but not beforehand. At the same time, we all have a somewhat vague feeling that we are looking for an ideal of perfection. The perfect rider, the perfect horse, the perfect relationship between the two. But what are these things?

In France, twenty years ago, when I was young, knowledge of the art of riding was out of reach of the ordinary person. It was something reserved for the older cavalry officers, something you were not supposed to know. Perfection was considered an impossible goal. But I had an incredibly powerful drive to get as close to perfection as possible. In my eyes, perfection was a good thing, and I worked hard for it. I tried to visualize it fully.

I was aware of the possibility of perfection very early in my life. My natural, childlike relationship with my horse was so special. It was the closest thing to perfection that was available to me.

I discovered that special situations helped the process. I used to ride with my eyes closed, or in the dusk, or late at night. There was no distraction, no noise—just the horse and me, all that was needed to be beautiful. This natural spirituality helped my educational process tremendously.

It was not until many years later that I even heard of the word "meditation" or realized that in those past situations I had put myself into a state of grace that allowed me to tap into cosmic energy, where cosmic knowledge became available to me. I believe now that all knowledge present and future already exists in a kind of open sea of cosmic intelligence that is available to those who are willing to try to tap into it with the power of the mind.

## VISUALIZATIONS
## ARE DRESS REHEARSALS

Everything that is created starts out as a thought in the mind. A brilliant and moving theatrical work begins as an idea in the playwright's mind. A massive, stunning sculpture, before it is born in bronze, or a painting, before it illuminates a canvas, is conceived as a vibration in an artist's brain. A chef starts planning a wonderful dish in his head before he begins to stew the stock and chop the carrots. The same thing is true of riding a horse with art and creativity.

The mental part of riding, however, has been overlooked and rarely spoken of, since riding a horse is thought of by many as a purely physical act. The mental part is something we have to put back into it, and we may have to make ourselves conscious of doing it for a time until it becomes more natural to us.

One way to do this is through visualization, a very powerful and useful tool to help you begin to move toward becoming the more effective rider you want to be. The wonderful thing about this technique is that you can practice it even when you are not on your horse; for example, while riding a commuter train or bus to work, or waiting in line at the post office.

Visualizations can be used as something like a mental dress rehearsal. You can create your goal as a rider, whether it is to execute an elegant and effortless *passage*, a flawless series of flying changes, or simply a perfect ten-meter circle at the trot, by visualizing yourself and your horse achieving them in your mind.

Visualization is more than just mental imagery; you have to include your feelings and sensations at the same time. Once this is done, sports psychologists say, our bodies do not distinguish the difference between real and imagined situations; physiologically they react to real and imagined situations in the same way. Champion skiers, tennis players, swimmers, golfers, and other athletes use this phenomenon to their advantage by running through a course or a game in their heads many times before they actually compete, imagining the moves they will make and picturing themselves victorious.

By creating a positive picture in your mind and then allowing your body to experience the event as if it were actually happening to you on your horse, you will be able to handle the real experiences with more and more ease, and progress more rapidly. If you imagine a situation often enough, it will already be familiar to you by the time you find yourself in it, and your body will respond with more relaxation and confidence than it would have otherwise.

Visualization is a picture in your head, complete with sound, smell, and feeling, of how the event is going to come out: a great warm-up, the perfect half-pass, or whatever it is you are going to work on. As I have said, learning time can be greatly reduced this way by practicing riding in one's mind while off the horse.

## VISUALIZATIONS
## TO INCREASE MIND POWER

Throughout this book, the reader will find visualizations that he can use to increase the power of the mind as the most important aid in riding. What follows is a list of a few that I have developed. Some are simple and have a more universal application. Others are more specific and are explained in-depth elsewhere in this book.

- *The double personality.* It can be useful to develop two personas that allow you to be more objective about your riding. You "watch" yourself ride in order to have less personal involvement when things become too intense and tend toward the negative. You can become even more removed if one of your personas becomes that of another person, such as your instructor. You "go" and sit by the wall and watch your instructor ride your horse.

- *The double mind.* You allow the horse to be aware of and to be in touch with one mind and not the other (see page 7). This can be useful in work such as flying changes. One mind says no, the other yes; this technique cures much of what people call anticipation on the part of the horse, and what I call reading the rider's mind. The horse cannot read the one mind you don't allow him to be aware of, and cannot anticipate the movement.

- *Turning the walls of the arena—a training technique that reinforces the horse's awareness of his balance.* In the sideways movements, for example, when a horse loses his balance in haunches-in, instead of correcting his balance the rider imagines that the walls of the arena have turned and asks the horse to go right into shoulder-in. By changing the movement, one makes the horse aware of his mistake, which the horse has to correct himself in order to perform the second movement. Education means making the horse more aware of what he is doing on his own. It is not the

24

horse responding to tricks from the rider. See page 142 for a more detailed explanation.

- *Work on the square.* The square is an important figure to use because people can visualize it more easily than they can a circle, as it has four corners and four straight lines. This makes it useful to mentally substitute the square for the circle at times. The shoulder-in on the square is an old technique which was developed by La Gueriniere. We see in old engravings that the "floor plan" for shoulder-in work is on the square. Work on the square is useful not only for the sideways movements but as a geometric figure.

- *Removing the walls of the ring.* The problem of a horse leaning in can be solved by sending your mind outside the ring. When the horse is leaning in you have to visualize that you are riding your horse outside the walls, meaning that you visualize the field, the paddock, the parking lot, or whatever actually exists outside the arena walls. Send your mind outside the wall so your horse visualizes that and not the wall. When the horse drifts out, meaning he is leaning on the wall, you have to visualize a much smaller circle than the one you are actually riding. See page 94 for a more detailed explanation.

- *Giant fingers—a way to exaggerate testing a young or green horse for self-carriage.* You exaggerate the giving motion when you drop the contact and then take it lightly back (see page 69). This makes it very clear to the horse that when you put your hand on the saddle, then move it forward in the direction of the horse's mouth, and then put it back on the saddle again, he is obliged to carry himself. It can be done with either the left rein or the right rein, or both. See the figure on page 26 to see how it is done.

- *Picturing a cliff right in front of you when you want to halt* (see page 34).

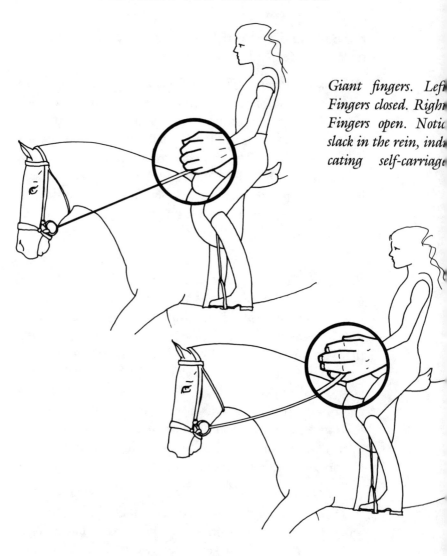

*Giant fingers. Left: Fingers closed. Right: Fingers open. Notice slack in the rein, indicating self-carriage.*

- *Visualization of somebody behind you chasing your horse with a whip, yet telling you to slow down, in order to achieve impulsion in collection.* Your body stays in the same passive position. Play with the fingers in order to allow the horse to stay in the correct mental and physical attitude (see page 40). Much as the hand of a good dancer is in contact with his partner, the rider's legs usually are in contact with the horse.

- *Visualization of a giant pulling a single hair up and back on top of a rider's head to get the rider's body in the correct position for collection* (see page 90).

- *If you want one good pirouette, imagine you are going to do two.* If you visualize one pirouette, generally the last two or three strides are going to lack quality. The visualization of two pirouettes allows the horse to believe he is going to carry on with the same movement twice; therefore it allows consistency in the movement from start to finish. See also page 134 for a more detailed explanation.

Riders who become accustomed to putting these visualizations into practice are likely to come up with their own creative discoveries.

## THE PERFECT HORSE

What is perfection in a horse? How many people know what it is or what it looks like? The perfect horse goes with "no hands," only the weight of the rein and a "breathing" leg on the part of the rider.

What must the rider's state of mind be to achieve this perfection? As I have said before, most of the time, I teach not riding, but communication between horse and rider. Human beings, due to the pressures of our civilization, have become less and less in harmony with animals. We have many difficulties in communicating with animals, so that riding has become diminished, a much lesser art than it was in past centuries. I find that many people, in order to ride well, must first heal their minds and spirits. They must rediscover their natural abilities and learn how to feel good in their own skins. The following meditation exercise may provide such healing and help improve harmony between horse and rider:

Put yourself in a very quiet place and meditate, visualizing your perfect horse. This is a very personal experience, so it will be different for everyone, according to his or her individual feelings and taste.

Ebauche de piaffer, *the beginning of the* piaffer: *Dom Pasquale, Quinta do Brejo* (PHOTO: FRANCINE HALKINS).

*Canter in lightness: Dom Pasquale, Lusitano stallion, at four years old, Quinta do Brejo* (PHOTO: FRANCINE HALKINS).

First, establish the setting. Perhaps a peaceful Kentucky farm with long pastures of green grass stretching to the horizon. Or a smooth-sanded beach along a sun-dappled sea at low tide, with just enough breeze to make it pleasant. An open green field bordered with tall weeping willows, and a pond just beyond, visible through the swaying branches. Or right at home in your own pasture. Any place that is appealing and comfortable for you.

Now for the horse.

Visualize the breed that you consider your perfect companion. That exquisite Arab, that sleek athlete of a thoroughbred, that spectacular, elegant *Selle Français,* or that regal, noble Lusitano is yours and alive . . . stallion, mare, or gelding, in a rich color of glowing chestnut, gleaming bay, or dramatic gray.

Now give him the soul of the perfect horse. Look at his large eyes. Fill them with generosity and honesty. He is looking at you. See his ears vibrating, turning, listening to you. Visualize his desire to communicate, his willingness to share and learn. What a warm feeling in your soul that gives you!

Visualize his walk, naturally long and regular, graceful, nearly catlike. Hear the sound of a perfect four-beat walk. See how his back is relaxed and swinging with the cadence of the walk. Close your eyes and *feel* that perfect walk.

Allow him to trot. You are sitting on a cloud, it is so light and smooth. He is truly on a circle, loose and relaxed, flexible. His feet do not seem to touch the ground. The rhythm is magical, mesmerizing, with a long, slow, regular, effortless stride.

His canter is a perfect three-beat canter, cadenced and round. Watch him in slow motion. What a stride, with lots of scope! Once again, experience it. Feel yourself sitting on him, completely passive, enjoying the clear feeling of a natural, round, stressfree canter. Can you also feel that deep enjoyment he has of his own free movement?

You have just experienced one of the most beautiful sensations in life, the perfection of complete sharing with another being.

Would you like to dance some more?

Imagine gliding into an easy shoulder-in. A fluent half-pass with steady rhythm, a consistent pirouette, a brilliant extension done in total relaxation. An effortless, cadenced *piaffer* and *passage*, done as if floating on clouds. Transitions are smooth, accomplished just by thinking and adjusting the lower back.

All movements are done in perfect balance, in perfect self-carriage by the horse, in perfect lightness, with reins made of silk thread.

This is the perfect feeling of harmony.

## THE PERFECT RIDER

What are some of the elements to be visualized in the perfect rider? Visualize the most aesthetically pleasing and effective riders that you know. Combine them and suddenly that is you.

I always try to put myself in the place of the horse whenever I think about the perfect rider. I ask myself: If I were a horse, how would I like the rider to ask me to walk, trot, canter, *passage*, or *piaffer* in the nicest way, without distress, without disturbing or interfering with me? When asked to walk, for example, if I were a horse, I would like first to be balanced in my halt, on the bit, collected, attentive to the desire of the rider, ready to reply to what he or she wishes of me. Then I would like the rider to ask me mentally, visualizing where he wants me to go, and which kind of walk he wants of me, and in what rhythm. Then, loosening his back, the rider says, "Let's walk now." No squeezing of my ribs with the legs, no driving seat or spur. The rider just lets the impulsion go through, like opening a tap and allowing the water to flow through.

Imagine a couple dancing. Do they need spurs and a half-halt to perform? No. They ask each other for what they want mentally most of the time, and it just happens. It should be the same with horse and rider.

## ATTITUDES
## NEEDED BY THE RIDER

Riding dressage is an *art de vivre,* a living art. If you are looking for a cooking recipe, a secret, or a trick, you are reading the wrong book.

One must ride a horse as one finds it. Horses have all the changeable qualities that human beings have. Treat them as equal beings. Try to feel and understand your horse physically and mentally on any given day, when he may be slightly different from the day before.

Your fingers will be the telegraph wires from your mind to the mind of the horse. Have as light a contact as possible. Just the weight of the reins: minimum contact, but with a maximum of control.

There is no secret to achieving this kind of contact—just an open and understanding mind. It requires a lot of work mentally, coupled with a lot of relaxation in your mind. Any sort of tension, mental or physical, will disturb the unity of the horse-and-rider pair.

The rider must be aware mentally of (1) his own feelings and attitudes, and (2) the feelings and attitudes of his horse. He must be physically aware of his body position and the horse's body position and of what would be the optimum interaction between them, with as much passivity on the rider's part as possible.

Generally, since body attitude reflects mental attitude, change your *mind* first—your body will follow. Completely relax your mind and body. Let go of the worries that you have at home or at the office. Create that very special little space in your mind where you are quiet, at peace, in communion, full of love and appreciation.

Be conscious of when you are in an optimum state of mental generosity and readiness to learn, or when you could be. Experiment. Ride the first thing in the morning sometimes if it offers more alertness, more awareness. Other times you might be more

31

relaxed riding at the end of a day's work. If you don't have the choice, make the best of what you have.

Your body should follow your mind and be completely re-laxed. Let it become an extension of the horse's body, part of it—your spine his spine, your breathing his breathing, his mind your mind: one body, one soul. Now you are ready to share. Be available to your horse: an open, vulnerable, giving, receptive rider, listening to a horse that is teaching you how he likes to be ridden.

This is reaching toward the ultimate, the highest expectation that can be conceived and realized, the perfect horse, the perfect rider, with perfect communion between the two.

Let's take impulsion as an example. Impulsion has to begin as a vibration in the mind of the rider before it becomes a phys-ical attitude. Learn to know your horse and impulsion will begin. Try the following meditation exercise.

Close your eyes and imagine that your very finest wishes are coming true. Visualize a magic walk. The rhythm is so regular, the impulsion so consistent. You do not have to do anything to get it. Those four beats just flow like a form of music.

You ask for a shoulder-in. Put your inside shoulder back, outside hand higher, and it happens. You give with the inside rein, and make it even more light for even more collection.

Visualize a flying change. To prepare, in general terms, put the horse in the physical position in which he will be able to do the flying change. Most important, find the rhythm and balance in which he will be able to do it successfully.

You prepare, you think about it, and it happens. The horse simply gives it to you. There is no stress. The horse is getting better with less effort, or from just the thought alone. Place your outside shoulder back, and your horse is in haunches-in just by visualization. The same for the pirouette or *passage*. This is per-fect harmony and the poetry of riding. This is beauty.

Mestre Nuno Oliveira once said, "There are two things in riding; technique and soul." The soul part is what we have nearly lost today and must put back into riding.

There is a French saying—*"C'est au moral du cheval qu'il faut d'abord s'attacher,"* meaning, "One must first be attentive to the mood of one's horse." The rider must analyze again and again behavior or reaction, but only *after* the ride. Let the intellectual, analytical part of your brain work before or after the ride. During your time on the horse, let your "animal" mind take over. Share feeling and sensation with your horse. The intellectual mind is necessary most of the time, but it can be a brake on progress if it is misused.

How can you tell when the intellect is taking over? It stops the feeling of togetherness, the unity of horse and rider. As you feel less and less response, you can be certain that you are working too hard at it, and unity is disappearing.

A good example is from my own personal experience. When I was seventeen, I stopped riding for nine months as soon as I made my decision to be a professional. My parents didn't know what to make of this. As soon as I had made that decision, I could not ride anymore. Until then, I was a natural rider to the point where I had nothing to analyze. I was unaware of the technical part of my ability. Now I tried to analyze everything I was doing. I wanted to know what made me a "natural." I lost the natural ability because I was working too hard at analyzing it.

After the experience, I discovered that I had to be analytical before and after, but not during the ride. That's when I came to the conclusion that it is common to put that intellectual part of one's brain between his body and the horse's, and communication doesn't work anymore. When you interrupt the communication, you kill the magic.

When you are actually riding, keep visualizing what you want, but do not let what I call the "intellectual mind" get in the way. You can overcome this tendency through relaxation, listening to the part of you that is really happy and willing to flow with something that feels nice. Meditate and enjoy the same feeling you get when being swept away by wonderful music without stopping to analyze it. It is letting the right side of your brain, the creative, intuitive side, take over completely. It can be difficult to overcome if you have a tendency to work too hard at things. This ability to let your entire self flow with things is actually not something one works at at all.

Always anticipate the horse's desires and his reactions. Simply offer your help in the direction of the best results. Ask for simple things clearly. This instruction may sound simplistic, but you might be surprised how many riders fail to do it, and how quickly this failure can be remedied with the help of a little visualization.

For instance, often when I am teaching, I will ask for a halt and the rider will protest that he or she is unable to stop the horse. I tell them, "Three feet ahead of you is a cliff. If you don't stop, you die!" My "cliff" works every time. I carry it with me everywhere that I give clinics.

One attitude that I find absolutely necessary in the rider is what I call the no-doubt mind. In clinics I use an anecdote about my dog, Spot, to illustrate what I mean:

In the kitchen of my brother's house in La Rochelle, France, there is one door and one window. Two situations can exist: In the first, the door is open and the window is closed. When my dog, Spot, a small Portuguese street dog of the terrier type, comes to the door under these circumstances and sees my brother's cat sitting on a chair in the kitchen, he will not attack it even though the cat is cornered. Although the cat is completely trapped, it knows it is superior and has only to resist my dog by mental power. Spot just looks at the situation and turns around and leaves.

Then we have the other situation, where the door and the window are both open. This creates a doubt in the mind of the cat. It knows it can resist mentally, but it knows it can fly out the window as well. My dog will attack it every time because the cat's mental focus is divided. Things similarly go wrong between rider and horse when the rider has mental doubts or an ambivalence about what he is doing.

Of course, any of these changes in you as a rider are not going to occur the first day. It will take time. Perfection is hard, very hard to achieve, because none of us is God. But everyone at his own level can get a little closer to it with each attempt. Sometimes just a circle in trot will give you a feeling of perfection, an effortless, timeless experience. Cherish the fine moments that do occur. They are rare, but they exist and come more often

*The smallest circle represents the center of gravity of the rider, the medium circle the center of gravity of the horse, and the largest the center of gravity of the centaur, the man and the horse together.*

and last longer, as time goes on.

I can give you a lot of don'ts to beware of in this process. Don't involve your ego or get tense in your mind and body, or be impatient to do too well too soon. Don't allow yourself to worry, or to ask for too much. Don't force the horse or bore him with a lot of unnecessary stuff. Don't kill the freshness and desire to please in your horse. Don't lose your own sense of humor or make what you are doing look like work. Don't take yourself too seriously.

Do feel your body as a unit. Feel all of your weight in the seat bones. Let yourself reduce or shrink to a little ball of fire and place it in your pelvic bones, which is your center of gravity when you ride. Center yourself there. Now imagine the same-sized ball of fire for your horse. Depending on his position and movement, that ball will remain more or less between his shoulder blades and to the rear of the withers. Finally, visualize a bigger ball of fire made by the two of you. This is the "we" that you have to play with, a very dynamic feeling. But that ball of fire can be very capricious! Treat it with a lot of tact.

Ask for a lot, expect only a little, and reward often. Be patient, and explain over and over again if needs be. When a problem arises, stop and start again—new horse and new rider.

## Part II

# A Training Approach: Beginning a Dialogue with Your Horse

# 4

# *Longeing*

If we want full results, all horses should be longed, then worked in hand, and then ridden. When we ride a horse, he is going to have to go forward on his own. There is no physical participation on the part of the rider—only mental participation. Longeing is where the horse learns that self-desire to go forward.

We longe a horse for many reasons. We want him to be more obedient and supple, we want to let him play at first and release excess energy. But the most important reason is to avoid even the thought of unnecessary fighting, which could create future problems.

Longeing is the beginning of the dialogue between horse and rider, in which you say, "Let's talk about things, let's communicate, let's decide if we want to dance together." It is what I call The Original Contract.

Before you sit on a horse, you want one that is already well tuned in to his rider, one that is 100 percent ready for you, because he will be correctly warmed up and in the right physical and mental frame. All the way through the horse's training, we are going to follow three steps in asking the horse to do anything, and always in the same order:

1. We are going to visualize, meaning that we mentally ask the horse to go forward.
2. We use a minimum of physical reinforcement of the visualization, using mostly the voice or the click of the tongue.
3. We use the whip. The horse must know that one touch of the longe whip means to go fully forward.

Never let the horse stop on his own in longeing. He must go when you want him to go.

The most common problem in longeing is that people do not have a very firm idea of longeing the horse forward in their minds. In Portugal, the way they longe young, or green, horses is to have a large man who holds the longe line stand in the center of the ring. A smaller man with a stick runs after the horses, and when this little man gets tired, another is sent in to take his place. You can visualize this while longeing your horse to help get the firm idea of having the horse go forward 100 percent.

You should have the psychological feeling of being behind the horse at all times when you are longeing him. Try to create the willingness for forward motion in the horse. Have the mental feeling that you are going forward with him.

Make longeing short and impulsive. If on a certain day the horse has a problem on the longe, be flexible. Longe him a little longer and don't ride him. It's better not to ride the horse when he is not correct than to create problems that will take weeks to solve. Above all, avoid a fight. Lots of longeing is useful in retraining a horse, as it brings about changes without fighting. Most problems can be solved very quickly from the ground.

Up to this point, the horse is being longed with a cavesson or the bridle. Once he is going forward, we introduce him very carefully to the side reins. I use the doughnut type with no elastic, which resembles the action of the human fingers on the reins. Put the side reins on as soon as possible to allow the horse to be in the correct position. Side reins only allow the horse to be correctly on the bit. Let the side reins do the hard work. They don't make mistakes.

As well as providing physical benefits, side reins are very important for mental understanding and communication. Side reins, by allowing the horse to be on the bit, allow the mental communication and visualization to work. However, there are a few *rare* horses that must never be longed with side reins, such as those who may have special back problems. The mental problems that result create more danger than the physical benefits. A horse with a weak back needs lots of slow longeing.

However, if the horse's back is really tight, he may rear or flip over backward if you start out abruptly with the side reins too short. If you have problems longeing with the side reins, it is possible that your lessons in going forward were not strong enough. I recommend that longeing be done under supervision if you do not have much experience at it. I usually start with one side rein long and low, generally at the level of the lower part of the saddlepad. (What I mean by long and low is that the side reins will be longer than they would be if they were placed higher. What you lose in height, you have to gain in length.)

Long and low, if the horse is resisting, will give him more room to learn and understand and not get hurt. If he fights the side reins, he will be able to pull them up and they will be too long for him to hurt himself.

When everything proceeds without problems, use both reins. Shorten and raise them up progressively, over time.

Always try to make your longe line slack; avoid establishing a steady contact with it. We want the horse to find his own balance without the contact of the longe line, to be independent of it and to have true self-carriage. If the horse pulls on the line, longe him in a corner and use the corner, which puts limits on where he can go, to create a slack in the longe line.

Sometimes it is helpful if you play a little with the longe line as one would play on the reins. To keep the horse feeling the outside rein, you can lightly (and momentarily) establish contact on the longe line in coordination with a push on the whip. That should make the horse rounder.

Depending on the temperament of the horse, he will, in time, find his own balance. He will discover it for himself, because that is where he likes to be. Progressively, the side reins are going to be slacker as the horse starts to find his own good position.

At the trot, really push the horse on the longe, so that he finds his own extended trot, really moving, but with a slow rhythm. Use lots of transitions. ("Really moving" means the lengthening of the stride; the rhythm is that in which he moves his legs. The horse that is relaxed and balanced is able to have a longer stride in the same rhythm. The horse that is not relaxed will go faster and generally shorter in stride.) Only a relaxed horse can extend properly. If a horse is asked to do a lengthening or extension in resistance, he will answer by doing a shorter, faster trot.

A dull, lazy, or unrhythmic horse will need a good, too active, too fast rhythm to start off with on the longe. Then let him slow down into the correct rhythm by himself. A naturally impulsive, nervous horse, however, will need very careful handling. The rider must use a lot of voice and tactful movements, carefully adapted to the problem. This type of horse will need more domination in order to make him trust the rider more, and to be able to think and understand. Once he gets over his initial block, get him into the correct rhythm. Through relaxation the rhythm will become slower. (Do not be overly preoccupied with rhythm at this point; rhythm will come later, as the horse relaxes.)

When the horse understands what is desired of him in longeing, there will be a different look in his eyes. His body will start to relax and the rhythm will become more regular. Reward him frequently.

You can test the natural balance of the horse at the canter by tightening the circle and watching his hindquarters. The unbalanced horse will flip his haunches to the outside. And the horse with natural balance will bring his haunches in closer to you on both reins.

Do not expect perfect results right away. A lot of things may happen on the longe line. You will possibly see some head tilting, problems in bending, canter-lead problems, cross-cantering, and haunches to the outside.

Head tilting is often produced by a problem in the horse's back. If the horse continually tilts his head, then the inside side rein has to be made shorter so the horse is looking in the direction in which he is going. In most cases, head tilting will be dealt with later in the training, during the work in hand and riding.

Most of the other problems also indicate a locked back, a stiffness or weakness due perhaps to old injuries. A locked back and stiffness can also be caused by mental problems. How can you tell which problems are physical and which are mental? One may never know. The mental and the physical are often interrelated. A horse may start out with a physical problem that proceeds to become a mental one. You try to do your best to know which is which, and experience helps. That's why professionals are needed. The work in hand is also helpful in showing which problems are clearly physical.

There are a lot of transitional periods in the longeing process. But when horses grow physically stronger, they get better on the longe. For instance, a horse that has been in the field for three years with his head up in the air will have a tendency to look overbent when he initially brings it down on the side reins. This is not a big problem but just indicates a lack of muscle necessary for him to hold his neck correctly. Ask for a lot of forward motion with long side reins until he builds up those muscles.

I do not recommend longeing before the horse is three years old. Always longe young horses with boots on their legs— galloping boots in the front and sometimes, if the horse interferes from the back to the front, use bell boots as well. Or the horse could be protected with polo bandages. I do not recommend exercise bandages because they are very difficult for people to apply and can create a lot of tendon problems. We are not looking for support but protection. When starting out the young horse, do only forward longeing and very active work in hand.

Your goal will be achieved when your horse is on the bit at the walk, trot, and canter, with no resistance. He will be happy in that position with slackened side reins.

All of the preceding is what I call basic work on the longe line. After that, you also have the possibility of working on extensions, collection, and on larger and smaller circles on the longe.

# 5

# *Work in Hand: The Golden Tool*

Work in hand is a very, very old technique that has been used from the beginning of the art of riding. Horses were big, powerful, and sensitive then. They were of a different type than we see today, coming basically from an Iberian or a Neapolitan background. And, of course, all riding horses were stallions because people at that time would not consider riding anything else.

In the time before cars and other forms of transportation, the number of horses that trainers had to deal with was absolutely incredible. They were forced to develop a method of training these horses that was very efficient. Work in hand, an important part of it, was a very popular technique. The last evidence of this old training method can be seen in the use of one pillar in antique dressage prints.

I think the way we practice work in hand today is very similar to the old technique. The rider or trainer who does the work in hand becomes a sort of movable pillar.

Work in hand is a very valuable tool for the trainer because one gets so much information from it. It should help you to decide how you are going to carry on with the horse's training. It will show you both the horse's weaknesses and strengths as well as give you an evaluation of the horse's mental and physical possibilities.

My first impression of a young, green horse will come from working him in hand; this is going to give me lots of information about him immediately. Number one, I see how he's built, or what his conformation is like; number two, I see how his conformation combines with temperament; three, how he moves; and four, how he feels about things. There is, of course, a strong relationship between temperament and conformation. A sour temperament usually means a very stiff horse because he works under stress. On the other hand, the happy-go-lucky guy is going to be loose and supple.

I will know if he's the type of horse that could charge at me, a horse that will challenge the basic contract of "let's work together." If the person working the horse does not realize the real challenge that such a horse is presenting him or her, and if he or she misjudges the problem, the trainer is susceptible to injury. With some horses, one has to proceed in a very low-key manner. One's approach has to be one of "Let's be friends and form a relationship first; we'll talk in detail later."

Work in hand is especially good for fearful horses that must learn to accept contact with the whip on their bodies without being frightened. They must realize that you do not use the whip as a punishment, never against them, always *for* them. The whip is there only to reinforce your mental message. It should be saying, "I'm talking to you, you did not pay attention to my mental message, my click of the tongue." It rarely says, "Bad boy."

Work in hand is also where a horse learns to keep out of your territory, the invisible circle of space, like an aura that you

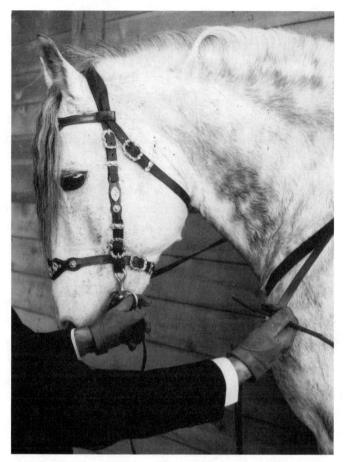

*Hand and whip position for work in hand* (PHOTO: MAURY COHEN).

have around you. Every creature in the animal world has his own space or territory, and if you go beyond that, you become the invader and you get into trouble. Man has somewhat lost that feeling, so you have to re-create your own space, a big circle around you that no one can enter unless invited. It keeps you from getting hurt by a horse that is swinging his head around and not thinking about respecting your territory.

When you are working a horse in hand and you come to a problem, try to make sure your breathing is in unison with the horse's. If you don't want a conflict, don't look him in the eyes.

That is an invitation to a confrontation. That is why you have to look at a horse's feet when you lead him into the trailer; you can never lead a horse if you look at him straight in the face. It's similar to what they say about meeting a bear in the woods: "Look at the feet of the bear." If you can manage not to establish eye contact, you will be in good shape. If you are sure you can handle the situation, then you can look the horse in the eyes. However, realize that you are going to have a fight. You need to know inside yourself that you are up for it.

Both with longeing and work in hand, I try to make sure that the horse is mentally and physically prepared for the rider. Mentally, when he accepts the dance with you, he accepts a sharing, fifty-fifty situation with you so that physically he is ready to do what you want him to do. Most of the problems I see occur when the horse is asked to share fifty-fifty, but a quiet "no" comes out of him, to which the rider doesn't pay any attention. He sits on the horse, and then, under all the mental stress of that "no," tries to make the animal do something that its body cannot do.

Work in hand must be seen in context with the rest of the training program. In proper sequence, the work in hand follows longeing the horse, first without side reins and then with them. Work the horse in hand as soon as possible after making sure he has accepted the side reins on the longe.

I do not recommend working in hand with side reins except in rare instances, such as with a seventeen-hand horse. In such a case I use them mostly for control, to limit the problem of the large horse throwing his head up and down, and even then I keep them very long.

Remember that on the longe, the horse should have learned to be really forward and in the correct position. He should be on the bit at the walk, trot, and canter. During transitions, the level of his head carriage should remain the same, and the horse should be pleased to be in that good position.

The horse continues to be taught during work in hand that he has to "go." You ask him to walk, and he keeps on walking until you ask him to stop. He is going to go in the rhythm that you want, and he is going to keep that rhythm until you ask him to stop. If you don't establish this idea while you are working in hand, you will spend all your time riding him by pushing, kicking, whipping, driving—all those things that we don't want to do because if we do them we can't do much of anything else.

Therefore, it's very important that the horse understands from the start that he has to work. Anytime he doesn't want to, give him a little touch with the whip to say, "That's your job, you can't do anything else."

Begin by establishing your position. The position of the trainer during work in hand is relative to how cooperative the horse is. When the horse does not cooperate, you have to be much more in front of him and slightly to the side. The more with you the horse is, the closer to the shoulder you can get while standing between the horse's shoulder and head.

At first you put the horse on the track, parallel to the wall. Your inside hand holds the bit, while the other hand holds the outside rein so that it crosses the base of the neck, in order that the entire position of the neck is controlled (see the figure on page 47). Keep an even bend throughout the body; too much bend in the neck will put too much weight on the inside shoulder. The whip is held in the hand that holds the outside rein. Some horses may react violently to it. When the horse is on the wall and if he is afraid of the whip, you have to massage his body with it so he learns he need not be afraid of it. He needs only to respect it.

When you "massage" the horse with the whip, you start by touching it along his neck and shoulder, going on to the front leg, and very carefully to the head, if he allows you to do that, and, tactfully, the back end of the horse. If the latter provokes some kicking or excitement, use your voice to calm and reassure the horse that you are not going to hurt him. Stay there and make your point that he has to accept it.

The horse needs to be in the same position he would be in on the longe line—on the bit, with the head at a height that "fits" straight, and with both hind legs underneath him. His back and front have to look connected. In some cases, you have to raise the head position in order for the horse to use his back. His jaw should be soft and relaxed, offering no resistance.

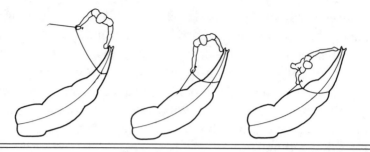

*The more control you need, the more in front of the horse you should be, as in #1. You may step more to the rear, as in #2, when less control is needed. #3 shows your position when the horse is mentally and physically with you.*

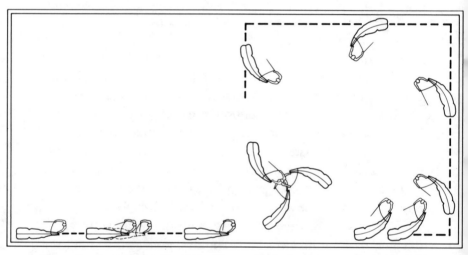

*You can do work in hand on the small circle, you can do it straight against the wall, or on the square.*
*#1. Going forward and backward against the wall.*
*#2. Doing a small circle.*
*#3. Passing through the corner and going on the square.*

Once the horse is in the correct position, ask for a simple halt. Then ask him to walk a few more strides and halt. There must be no argument about it. He is between you and the wall and he can't go anywhere. You do not lead the horse. He has to go forward from your mind, voice, or whip. Let the horse make the first move, not you. You will need to make a longer than normal stride, because the horse has a longer stride than you have. Go forward along the wall: one, two, three steps, then back: one, two, three steps. Use fewer physical aids each time.

Repeat this exercise until it becomes easy. It sounds simple, but you'll discover it isn't when you actually try it with a horse. Horses do not want to be between the trainer and the wall. The trainer must look for a consistent, regular rhythm. If the horse has problems, he will tend to hurry.

At this point, work in hand represents very strong domination. I don't mean *domination* as most mean it—"me first, and you never." My interpretation is more like, "We will do this fifty-fifty," or "Will you dance with me?" with the proper response being a polite yes. It is acceptance of sharing.

You will sometimes have problems with the horse tilting his head. You have to make sure you are in control of the outside rein, so the bend is regular from the head to the tail. If the horse opens and closes his mouth nervously when being worked in hand, it means stiffness in the back and shoulders. If so, work the horse on a small circle. In the stiff horse, work for flexibility first, then get his nose down. Work the stiff horse in hand, right and left, back and forth, until the moment he relaxes. (See the figures on page 50, for illustrations of these elementary exercises.)

Next, make the horse go around you in a circle (see the bottom figure on page 50). You act like the ancient pillar; you walk very little and make the horse move around you as if you were a movable pillar. Basically, you want a position that is close to the shoulder-in. You want both front and back legs to cross. The trainer should use the wall to maintain the correct shoulder-in position, if necessary.

The work in hand will, as I have mentioned, reveal a horse's irregularities. The horse may have seemed perfectly happy to work on the longe line, moving straight and on a small circle. But once you ask him to cross his legs, you may see problems with his shoulders, hind legs, or back. He may prefer to stop with one hind leg to the rear, or he may drag one hind leg or block one

51

shoulder. All this gives you an indication of the horse's true form, exactly how he uses himself, what he does with his weight and balance, and what your future work with him is going to be.

Most important of all, be patient. Never get on a horse that you cannot stop. Do work in hand first. Work in hand gives you the ability to stop the horse whenever you wish. Establishing such control is crucial if you are to have a safe working relationship with your horse.

I would not attempt to train any horse without working him in hand. Most of the training I do, 60 percent of it at the lower levels, is just basic work on the flat. It is teaching the horse to know where his legs are. Work in hand is also very useful before and after trailering to supple and relax the horse after the stress of the trip or competition.

Don't be afraid to try this effective technique. An inexperienced person will not harm the horse by attempting work in hand. That is the beauty of it. If the person is calm and knows what he wants to do, he will do no damage whatsoever. It could work less effectively, but with practice it should improve.

The responsibility of a teacher is to give tools to students that they can use and not easily misuse. Work in hand is a great tool because you cannot easily do damage to the horse.

Some people use work in hand for the beginning of the *piaffer,* which can be done effectively too, but it is more specialized work which will not be described in this book.

Once again, it is important for the person working the horse in hand to have a clear understanding of what he is trying to achieve. Most people work their horses without understanding what they are working toward. They don't have a goal in mind. It is important to visualize, to have a picture with movement and with feelings in your head of what you wish to accomplish.

It is difficult to recognize the problems that you are experiencing and to say, "Today I expect this much improvement to happen." And as soon as that is accomplished, say, "That's great; I got what I wanted," and then quit.

# 6

# *Working with the Nature of Your Horse*

In training a horse, you have to work with the nature of the animal you have. The way the training is going to proceed will depend on the temperament and the conformation of every individual horse. They will be different for every horse.

Through longeing, your goal is to create a relationship with your horse, so that anytime you ask him to use his energy, he will. Remember how the longeing is done in Portugal, with a little man running after the horse with a whip in his hand? This impulsion always has to be in the mind of the horse; he always has to have the image of a little man ready to come out and run after him with a whip. He should not be frightened of it, but, in the case of the lazy or ungenerous horse, you may have to use the whip a little more often. Ninety-nine percent of the problems you will have in longeing will come from loss of impulsion. You will have lost the little man running after the horse.

In automotive terms, what you need is a Porsche. Suppose you think that what you have is an old truck. There need not be any old trucks. Any horse can be converted this way into a Porsche.

To make another comparison, imagine an electrical generator and think of the voltage that you want. That voltage has to be strictly mental, with as little help as possible from the physical. All through the training you are going to minimize the physical use of the whip. It is not how much or how hard you use it that actually counts. It is the mental message that you send with it. If the old truck reappears, go back in your mind to the Porsche, and if it is not there, you had better stop everything until you get the Porsche back. The power has to come before everything else. Then the relaxation follows. If you have to repeat a lesson, do it by starting again from the very beginning, from step one.

You have to override the slow horse, make him go faster than he wants to, and then tune him down to his own rhythm. And vice versa for the nervous horse; you have to make him sluggish first, then allow him to go up again into the proper rhythm for him. The reason is that if you are always trying to make the nervous horse slow down, or the lazy one go faster, then each will hate you because you are going against his nature.

If a horse is overproducing energy and you find you have a twelve-cylinder Ferrari, more than what you need, you have to reverse the system you used on the old truck. You act as a sponge. Put the needle on your electrical generator down to zero and decelerate, suck up all the energy, drain off the extra, and pour in relaxation. You are using your own nervous system as an electrical generator as you bring the power up or down as needed. Relaxation is the negative pole; it is a balancing effect you are after. Whatever you want to achieve, *you* have to be at the other pole to balance it.

If you have a problem with nervousness in the horse, you must try to relax him, try to make him sluggish. You must always seek a balance between extranervousness and relaxation. You try a little harder, or ease off a bit, to find the proper mixture. Don't worry about the movements or rhythm at this point. When you work on impulsion, don't worry about rhythm. It's when you work on relaxation that you will think about rhythm. Rhythm helps a lot in relaxing the horse because of the interrelationship between rhythm and balance.

Rhythm is very important because if the rhythm changes, the balance changes, and vice versa. When the horse's balance is constantly changing, you can't have relaxation. If the balance changes because of tension, then the rhythm will change. The rider helps the consistency of the balance through visualization of rhythm.

However, if you look only for rhythm in a nervous horse and don't care about relaxation, relaxation will never come. Relaxation has to come first in a nervous horse because he has too much uncontrolled impulsion or energy. In a lazy horse, it is impulsion that must come first.

Once you have that ball of fire going forward on the longe, you have to channel it. That's where "on the bit" becomes important and adjustment of side reins comes into the picture, so that the horse keeps his impulsion in a good position.

What about brakes? The brakes are not there during longeing. What we have is "go, go, go." The brakes will come in the stage of work in hand.

# 7

## *The Pieces of a Puzzle*

This is perhaps a good place to review what we mean by certain terms, all of which fit together like the pieces of an interlocking puzzle in the way they work and finally form the whole picture of the trained horse.

*Collection* is not, as it is so widely thought, just another exercise that happens or begins at a certain level of competition, generally accepted to be third level. Collection is the ultimate goal of training. To collect a horse means to invite him to put himself into a shortened frame that allows him to move forward, backward, sideways, and even upward, in the most optimum time possible. Collection is a natural defense mechanism of the horse. He gathers himself and takes off in the direction opposite to any danger with which he is confronted. Classically, collection is the characteristic of *l'Équitation d'École,* or "High School riding." In the training of a young horse, it is not that mysterious thing that has to happen after lengthening. It is an absolute misconception to believe that any lengthening comes about *before* collection. I wish the inventors of modern dressage tests would study the classics, or train a number of horses themselves and allow the horses to teach them about collection and what the natural progression is.

I am amazed to see young, gifted riders with talented horses win in first level, before collection is officially supposed to be achieved. They are mainly self-made, natural riders. A natural, loving rider has a gift of his or her own, the gift of noninterference. Very soon, with the help of pseudoexperts, the harmony and beauty of the pair is done in as the rider is taught to interfere.

Riders who do not have this natural gift must first learn to be passive, and then try, if needed, to help improve the communication without upsetting the horse. This is admittedly very difficult, even for the most knowledgeable, talented *écuyer.*

Collection is a consequence of the "on the bit" attitude, the most basic principle in dressage, but one that few riders today truly understand.

*On the bit,* as I define it, is the mental and physical attitude of a horse willing to share fifty-fifty with you, accepting you 100 percent. This is the neutral or original physical attitude of a horse that has a basic awareness of his body and a mental agreement to try to do his best. He has been mentally prepared and is willing to perform as a consequence of a relationship developed through longeing and work in hand. The horse is mentally comfortable and able to perform such basic suppling exercises as shoulder-in. Then, with a rider mounted on his back, the horse learns a different balance and a different awareness of how to carry a passive body on his back.

*Le ramener* is the head and neck position of the horse. Every horse has a basic head and neck position that allows his back to work and the whole horse to be connected. *Le ramener* is individual for each horse. We begin to discover through work in hand the level of the head carriage that, in relation to the horse's back, is optimum for every specific work and degree of training.

One of the most crucial decisions for the rider is to fit the horse's front with his back at a precise time, because there is no articulation between the horse's spine and his shoulders. That position starts from the hind legs and the hind legs only. The degree of *le ramener* changes depending on the engagement of the hindquarters.

Know when to elevate the front; make sure the back is strong enough. Elevate the front when you think the back end of the horse is supple and strong enough to take it. (See the figure on page 87.) Here is where we have what for me is the connection or interrelationship between *le ramener* and collection. Forcing a horse into collection is very bad because his back may not be strong enough to take it. Collection is not compression; it is the balance where everything is easy for the horse to do.

*Engagement* of the hindquarters is the ability of the horse to position his hind legs under his body, to distribute his weight from the front to the back, and to sustain such a balance with optimum freedom from the rear. Of course, the engagement of the hindquarters depends on how much the horse is sitting on them, how low he is in back. If he's sitting too much, there's no movement possible, as in the *levade*. He can't go forward. If he is not low enough, the maximum of collection can not be obtained.

*Le ramener,* together with engagement of the hindquarters, gives us collection, which in French we call *le rassembler*. The horse will not truly engage if he is not basically supple, free of stress, on the bit, and in a state of lightness. The stress can be physical, from the rider who is using a pushing seat or a compressing, tense, or gripping leg. Or the stress can be mental, when the rider does not know precisely what he wants and is not communicating with the horse.

There is much misunderstanding about *impulsion*. The golden rule is to have the minimum of impulsion necessary for the movement that we want to perform in complete relaxation. Today we see too much speed and running around in the wrong position passing for impulsion. We need a controllable impulsion

59

coming from an aware horse that is in communication with the rider. We need enough impulsion to maintain first the horse's position, and second the movement. However, that impulsion is destructive if the horse is not on the bit or is working against relaxation. But if there is not enough impulsion, what you do have is useless; what a rider needs is the perfect mixture between nerve and relaxation to create the movement. Once again, only the mind of the horse will be able to maintain the level of impulsion necessary to perform. He needs no interference from the rider.

True impulsion is completely dependent upon *flexibility*, which is the mental ability of the horse to use his suppleness to the maximum if he's asked to bend and use his ankles, hocks, and other joints.

Flexibility in the horse depends a great deal upon his having a positive mental attitude. Your horse can be supple, but if his mind is not at ease, he cannot be flexible. A horse must be mentally willing to use his physical suppleness. We cannot compare *willingness* and submissiveness as defined in the rules of competition. Submissiveness, that is, the horse not resisting the rider, is only the first step toward our goal. Willingness is the desire of the horse to do something. If we ask for more impulsion, a horse without flexibility will give us movements that are stiff. Flexibility is the only thing that makes impulsion controllable.

*Conformation* of the horse is not as important as people think. More important is how his mind allows his body to move. I have seen many top conformation horses so mentally contracted that they could not use themselves properly. The reverse is also true. A horse with mediocre conformation can be a superior mover; because of his very willing mind, he can overcome his conformation defects.

Classically, *lightness* was a consequence of flexibility. Baucher defined it as perhaps also the cause. I will not enter into that controversy. It depends on the horse; sometimes one will come before the other.

Sometimes *le ramener*, with the relaxation of the jaw, comes first, then engagement of the hindquarters, then true collection in lightness. Sometimes engagement comes first, then the relaxation of the jaw. The roundness of the horse is important, whichever part comes first.

Classically, the horse engages his hindquarters and then he relaxes his jaw, then the collection comes in lightness. I prefer engagement to come first; it is a sign that the horse is more of a "natural," of which only about 20 percent are. We do know that impulsion, flexibility, lightness, and engagement are interconnected, all actually becoming one thing.

Lightness is vital, a *sine qua non*; without it the horse and rider can have nothing else. The horse must keep an effortlessly correct attitude, mentally and physically, without any effort from the rider. Lightness is mental and physical self-carriage. Put your horse in a position and tell him, "Stay there." The way to keep him there is to find the perfect balance between impulsion and relaxation, a position in which he's comfortable. When you put a horse in that position, he does not move from it until he's asked. As soon as the movement is correct, concentrate on the lightness; let the horse do it on his own.

You may have to spend two or three months of your life impressing on your horse that he's never going to change position or attitude on his own—a very important aspect of the training. If he changes attitude all the time, the shape of the pieces of your puzzle changes all the time, making the completion of the picture impossible. If his rhythm changes, then his balance changes; it is like running in circles.

You must insist, "If I don't want change, you don't change!" It is very similar to when you learn to dance with a partner, knowing where you are relative to him or her at all times. Acquiring this mental cooperation from your horse may seem like an improbable, even impossible, goal. It takes a positive mental attitude on the part of the rider to achieve it.

This is the part that you will not find in books, even reading between the lines in the classics. Because of the era in which those classic masters lived, it is very difficult to learn the truths of riding through their books. Everybody had different concepts but used the same words, a problem of semantics. At the same time, they could not give the horse his due, the role he deserved. In other words the masters could not acknowledge mental communication with the animal unless they wanted to be burned at the stake as witches.

Perhaps they were not conscious, or did not want to be conscious, of having the complicity of the horse. The classic masters denied these natural feelings, but that doesn't mean they didn't have them. Because they were masters, their talent made up for it.

# 8

# The Physical Preparation of the Positioning of the Horse, and the Mental Attitudes of the Rider

## PUTTING THE HORSE ON THE BIT

This entire book is about putting the horse on the bit, such a fundamental concept that it is covered at every level, beginning to end.

Putting the horse on the bit is the foundation stone for the relationship with your horse. There is no, or very little, communication without it. Before anything else, the horse must be on the bit. On the bit is the position for communication—his balance is correct, the horse is listening.

Only attempt putting a horse on the bit after longeing him and doing work in hand. In order to allow yourself to sit on the horse, you make sure he is physically able and mentally willing to be on the bit. Put the horse on the bit as soon as you sit on him.

Let him know exactly where you want his nose, then lighten your hands and let him be comfortable while letting him maintain his head position on his own. By no means let him put weight in your hands; give him the responsibility of carrying his head.

Make your first attempts at the halt when you can make yourself understood more easily than when you are moving at the walk. Some horses will find it easier at the walk. If you can do it at the halt it is better, because if there is no movement, then balance will be no problem. Make sure your mental image of what you want is strong and clear.

If there is a need for more impulsion, one can make the first attempt at putting the horse on the bit during the walk. Does a horse show impulsion at the halt? Yes, just as a steam engine does. The steam is there even though the train is not going anywhere. You can stop the train, but you still have steam in the engine. The horse must have the desire to go forward, although at the moment he is standing still.

Stop on the wall with the horse on his easy (more comfortable) side. Your legs softly in contact, shorten the reins and place your hands on the saddle (right in front, on the highest part of the saddle) in order to prevent any backward movement of the hands. Apply light pressure with fingers and legs until the horse gives, drops his head, relaxes his lower jaw, and bends his haunches. As soon as the horse gives to you, you also give by opening your fingers. At times try to give first, and see if the horse will give to you then.

Then, at the walk, try to keep the horse on the bit by playing with your fingers. As soon as the horse resists by putting his head up, stop and repeat the exercise, and then walk again.

Afterward, still at the walk on the horse's easy side, think about the position of shoulder-in. To do the shoulder-in, position the horse by just looking where you want to go, with your outside hand higher and your inside shoulder back. (See chapter 18. As I have said, all these little parts of the puzzle are interrelated—one can use the shoulder-in to put the horse on the bit.)

Then reverse and try the same technique on the horse's harder side. Then reverse again. Get a good walk on the bit before attempting the trot. Work on at least a minimum amount of lightness by playing with the fingers before attempting the trot on the bit.

The elements you are looking for in on the bit are lightness, a high-quality relaxation, a general roundness and bend in the haunches, and having the horse with you 100 percent mentally and physically.

We will go into the concept of on the bit and its application in much greater detail in "Working Systematically" (chapter 13).

## THE CONCEPT OF THE FIXED HAND AND THE TECHNIQUE OF PLAYING WITH THE FINGERS

Before talking about the fixed hand, we have to understand the relationship among *le ramener* (the French term for the head and neck position of the horse), the length of the rein, the fixed hand, and the role of the elbows as a reflection of the upper part of the body on your hands. This relationship is similar to a big puzzle with pieces that dynamically change shape with the movement of the horse. These pieces may change all the time, but the rider still has to find a way to make them fit together.

*Le ramener* depends on the conformation of the horse. The degree of *ramener* depends on a particular movement (such as the shoulder-in) and is determined by the frame necessary for the attitude of the horse during that movement.

Correct rein length is very important, since it allows optimum and maximum use of the rider's hands. Rein length is the conscious decision of the rider to determine the space that the horse needs to position his head and neck for a given attitude.

### The Fixed Hand

The fixed hand is a hand that is not allowed to move, but that *moves with*. A French expression regarding this concept is *bouger sans bouger*, which means "moving without moving." The hand does not stop the impulsion. Another French saying is "you do not cork the horse's mouth." One allows the impulsion to go through, with the hands acting as a filter.

Put the horse on the bit with your shoulders back and your hands on the saddle, so that the hands play the role of side reins. (We don't need to use the leg in the beginning as we are using the natural desire of the horse to go forward.)

There is a huge amount of difference in contact between hands on the saddle and "floating" hands. Even when contact is momentarily too strong, with hands on the saddle at least there is a hope for lightness, while with floating hands there can be pulling.

Your elbows should always stay at your sides. Follow the horse's mouth with your back, not with your hands, as the Mestre Oliveira always used to say.

## Playing with the Fingers

*Why You Use It.*  Playing with the fingers is very much like transmitting signals through a radio channel, allowing ongoing communication between horse and rider. Because we use minimum leg and hand action, and very little seat, playing with the fingers has a very important role in creating and aiding mental communication between horse and rider, establishing this communication, and keeping it alive.

Since every horse is different, and each side of the horse is different and will change in time and space, this must be a dynamic activity on the rider's part. Playing with the fingers, like the radio channel, should allow for two-way communication. There should be a constant exchange of feeling, especially as regards feedback from the horse.

When you ask for a bend, for example, something is going to happen. If it is done properly and you've done your homework, it should work. Perhaps you will feel a resistance, and you must determine if it is mental or physical and then do something about it.

Whether it is mental or physical is one of the most delicate questions there is, even for top professionals. The more you work with horses, the more you can figure out which is which, through experience, knowledge, and a lot of reflection. But you have to understand that most of the time most people don't even consider the options.

Of course, mental and physical problems are very much interrelated. When the horse has a mental problem, it is going to show up as a physical one, and vice versa. If it is a physical problem, it may be the result of overpositioning: too much bend, and the horse says no. If it is mental, go back to your "homework" of longeing and work in hand.

*How You Use It.* The expression "playing with the fingers" means a very quick, sensitive opening and closing of the fingers of one or both hands, coupled with a very important mental message, whatever the message may be. For example, the closing of the fingers when the horse is trotting on the bit can mean, "Put your nose down," and when the horse's nose is already down, the opening of the fingers can mean, "Thank you, you're in good position. Stay there and be light." Closing the fingers can also mean a little more bend, left or right.

Opening the fingers must always be looked at as a reward. Closing is less important than opening. The perfection of *descente de main* (no hands), when achieved, is the constant opening of the fingers, the horse being "on parole," if I may say that.

Perfect contact is the weight of the reins alone; that, with our goal of *descente de main* and *descente de jambe,* should lead you to the goal of having your hands more often open than closed. Closing is only a gentle reminder, as I have said, of whatever the mental message is. The horse does not need the contact of the closed hands to perform.

One of the goals of playing with the fingers is that, by allowing no contact with the mouth of the horse beyond the weight of the rein, it makes leaning and pulling by the horse impossible. In other words, the reins become mentally nonexistent for the horse as a physical aid he can lean on. The horse cannot pull on nothing. Being quick with your fingers and not letting any weight come into the hands mean that playing with the fingers therefore allows for, and sometimes produces, lightness.

Riders always ask, "How do you use playing with the fingers?" There are no rules here. It is a vibration. Whatever works, works. You can use both hands at the same time, in rhythm with the movement or not in rhythm. *However, never have the same contact on both reins.* As soon as equal contact is established, the horse can lean on the bit. (That is why the double bridle is so beautiful, because the horse cannot lean on one bit—there are two of them.)

*When You Use It.* Once you have the correct length of rein (see also chapter 10, on balance), then you use playing with the fingers for the following:

1. to put the horse on the bit
2. to keep the horse on the bit
3. for a light bend, making sure your outside rein allows this bend
4. for lightness

The timing and the quickness of the fingers is very important, considering that the horse is faster in his reactions than most humans are. Prevent his leaning on the bit before it happens, with the constant playing of the fingers.

## A VISUALIZATION
## THAT TESTS FOR SELF-CARRIAGE

One of the most common faults I see in riders is what I call the double pull. This occurs when during both the closing and opening of the fingers the rider pulls on the reins. In other words, you still have contact there. It is important that when you open your fingers the contact is dropped completely to allow true self-carriage.

Over the years, in testing for the self-carriage of the horse in this way, I have developed what I call giant fingers. When I purposely put my hand forward in the direction of the bit, to allow for true self-carriage and put him "on parole" momentarily (if you will), I visualize a giant hand with enormous fingers. This image easily exaggerates the movement of giving toward the horse's mouth. Then I come back to the original position on the saddle, which makes the message for the green horse easier.

It is very important never to do this with the "right rein, left rein," in rhythm with the gait, because the horse will start to follow and nod its head and wave it in anticipation of the movement. (Seesawing, or taking contact with the mouth of the horse and pulling left and then right, is something totally different, and never appropriate.)

# 9

# *Visualization for Producing Energy or Impulsion*

A problem that I often see is that the rider wants to dance with the horse and yet never tells the horse about it. One must tell the horse what's happening. The energy has to come from the horse himself, and the way to get it is through mental visualization. You need a Porsche or a Ferrari; you can't ride around in the old truck. The horse needs to be sharp. You set the rules and say, "Guess what? You have to be 100 percent willing to get on with it. You are going to be 100 percent with me." If you want the horse to use himself 100 percent, it is never good if you force him, because how can he actually give 100 percent when he is resisting?

To get impulsion, imagine you are creating or releasing champagne bubbles in a beautiful crystal glass.

If you have a really lazy horse, one that has a tendency not to pay attention to you, as if nobody is at home, imagine that the roof of the barn is falling in and you have five seconds to get out of the ring. (That's the kind of energy you have to summon when you ride—your horse is going to *piaffer* or gallop, or at least wake up.) Know what level of energy you need for a specific horse at such a time. Go back to the image of the generator, with a needle that can go up or down. If 10,000 volts are produced, you have to learn how to regulate the energy. Sometimes you have to act like a sponge, to absorb the extra energy that is produced by a nervous horse.

A fundamental part of your relationship is that your horse must enjoy his work and want to give you the maximum. Fortunately, horses are basically willing to cooperate and do the best they can do for you. Through training, you refine that desire.

In creating this complicity, matching horse and rider is very important. Generally, people who have problems in real life pick problem horses to make sure they don't succeed. I see this happen very often. This is why I say horses are karmic. The harder you try to produce impulsion physically, the less it is going to work.

I repeat again, because it is so important, what the French master Baucher said: "Make yourself understood, and let it happen." Reading between the lines of that statement, one realizes the implication that the majority of responsibility for performing is up to the horse.

What is important in riding is not so much your body's athletic ability; it is your relationship with your horse. I see people who are actually physically handicapped, but who, because of their positive feelings, have high rates of success and wonderful relationships with their horses.

# 10

# *Balance*

For centuries, the *écuyer* (riding master; *le grand écuyer* was the title held by the riding master of the king) has tried to find and analyze the balance of the horse, and then tried to change this balance.

At the time of Baucher, in the mid-1800s, balance was synonymous with the center of gravity. Baucher said that when it feels right, it is right. On that point every *écuyer* agrees.

To begin at the beginning, the horse has what I call the original balance, which is not necessarily what God gives the horse. It is the basic balance that is the foundation stone for all you will do that is effective. Whatever you do, you will come back to it because it is a spot where you and the horse are in the perfect mental and physical position. After any problem that you may have, you will return to that position.

How one recognizes this original balance comes from seeing a lot of horses, which is another reason you need a professional trainer who has knowledge and experience. The trainer visualizes the balanced horse, closing his eyes and seeing how that horse could look when its training is finished, much as a painter or a sculptor does when he envisions a finished work before he picks up his brush or chisel.

Balancing a horse comes very close to being a creative act. Knowledge of balance is an aesthetic judgment on the part of the trainer. Some people have that judgment, others will learn. One kind of knowledge you have when you look at a particular horse from the ground. Based on past experiences that you have had with horses of different shapes, you have a vision of what the horse should look like. Then, when you sit on him, you try to adapt that vision to the real possibilities of the horse actually being in that position. Sometimes you are deceived by what you sit on. Sometimes your feeling reinforces your preconceived vision. Or sometimes the vision is absolutely shattered, and you may have to work toward something else.

You will have to teach the horse to find his balance and stay in it before you sit on him, through longeing and work in hand. However, when you do sit on him, you will find that things change.

Once again, when you sit on your horse, you will visualize that original balance you want him to have as you ride him. Every time you sit on the horse, you are going to put him in that position. You are going to make it better, but you must start with this original balance. This is not a static balance; it is going to improve.

On a spiritual level, the original balance position is your meditation spot. It is a space in which the horse and you are physically and mentally comfortable.

This is where my thinking differs from that of other trainers. The latter always consider the horse wrong, and they want to make it right through tricks. My goal, however, is to start out correctly and keep the horse correct, not constantly correct him. I am not going to totally rebalance the horse all the time. I want to put my horse in a correct balance, leave him there, and hope he is going to stay there, all of which implies passivity on the rider's part. You must encourage self-balance by the horse. I don't want him to think I am in charge of his balance; he is.

The rider is like the feather on the nose of the circus clown. It takes very little movement from the tip of the feather to make the big clown move. That's the basic thinking behind the "less is more" theory in riding. In the same way, a light touch with the whip or leg will make the horse move. It is psychological. You do not make the horse move by pushing with the leg or seat.

The horse has to want to dance with you. It is part of the fifty-fifty proposition to which you agreed in the beginning. "You do your part," you tell the horse. The rider simply suggests things, which is what education is. Your horse will know himself when he is balanced. Otherwise, it is like a dance in which one partner makes a mistake and the other hits him in the teeth. The first doesn't know why, because it was never explained to him! If you constantly correct the horse's balance, you are saying, "You are a dumb dancer. I'm not going to tell you anything, but if you make a mistake, I'm going to kick you in the teeth."

All we have in that partnership is mutual incomprehension, with no communication. As far as I know, this mental attitude has never been thought out or verbalized before, but it exists. It's terrible, and it's not education.

I have noticed that the talented rider has the gift of nonintervention. He puts a horse in the position the horse likes best to do a certain movement. After that, the rider tries to visualize it in as classical a manner as possible. The gifted rider does this, but he doesn't talk about it. Before I tried this approach, everything I did either didn't work, or if it did, it was ugly. Even when I succeeded, the result was nevertheless unaesthetic.

Dressage is the systemized method of improving the balance of the horse through different levels of training. In other words, it is not static, but dynamic. It is what makes a horse trained. At the beginning, you and the horse have that good balance that has already taken him off the forehand, and then progressively it becomes an educated balance as the horse gets more into collection (off the forehand and onto the hindquarters). On a horse with educated balance, you must have the feeling you can *piaffer* anytime you want to. It is comparable to the difference between the ability of a novice dancer and that of a trained one.

Good balance is related to rhythm, so you must find the right rhythm for the horse. Most of the time, the less one does, the better and the more relaxation one can achieve. Balance should come naturally.

Ask for as much balance as you can with minimal interference with his relaxation from the very beginning. Ask yourself, what is the best balance I can get without disturbing him mentally?

Your horse may become nervous about it when you first ask him. He may get tense, and there will be less impulsion as a result. The steam, the energy, is going to come through the horse only if his mind allows it to—that's what flexibility is. The horse's brain allows his back to move. The unbalanced horse is tense both in his mind and body. He is like a person skiing in the wrong position—his legs are going to ache.

Most problems that occur with a horse's balance come from the rider. The horse may have his own original mental or physical problems, but they are rare. If you take care of them at the beginning, you are ahead of the game. Ask very little, and reward frequently. It is a good idea never to disappoint your horse mentally by asking him for something he can't do. It is like betraying a friend.

The art of balancing a horse comes from knowing how much you can do without disturbing his relaxation. Otherwise, the horse locks his jaw and locks his back. Most people find ways to fight these resistances, which should not even be there in the first place. That is why your hands should not be pulling on the rein, or your legs banging against your horse (especially with spurs), as these are actions that upset a horse.

You always have the opportunity of stopping when something goes wrong, then starting anew with a "new rider" and a "new horse." Forget all past histories. If you stop and reexplain, what you want is going to happen. As Baucher said and as I often repeat, "Make yourself understood and let it happen." Go back to the original contract: "I want to dance with you."

True resistance comes when the horse ignores this contract and says to you, "I don't want to talk to you, I don't want to dance with you." A false resistance occurs when, for example, the horse resists the shoulder-in, but is actually saying to the rider, "It's not comfortable, could you ease off, could you do it in a slightly different position?" Then you have to modify things. You have to know each other well enough to distinguish the difference between these resistances. The degree of relaxation is the barometer. As soon as something is wrong and the horse grows tense, analyze again. Learn how to listen to your horse, as he will tell you how he likes to do things. That's how you create the mental space where he can do the movement. Remember what your original contract is when you ask, "Do you want to dance with me or not?" We don't invade the horse's space when we do this; we ask him whether he wants to share his space with us. Mestre Oliveira would say, "You have to know how to change a horse's balance; if you know that, you can do whatever you want."

There are many different balances for different purposes, which we will explore further in chapter 16.

# 11

# *Collection in Lightness*

Through lightness, equestrian art is capable of being one of the most perfect experiences of beauty. What is better than to perform a High School movement, a *passage* or *piaffer,* with the horse truly collected, truly light, with maximum impulsion and a slack in the rein? Then the horse starts to live, to give himself, and one can speak of brilliance, beauty, panache, art, or of *"La belle légerté à la française"*—the beautiful, French-style lightness.

If one has never felt lightness, it is a difficult concept to understand. Lightness is a must in achieving true collection; collection *is* maximum impulsion in lightness. If you try to collect the horse with any sort of strong contact in the reins, what you are doing is compressing, not collecting. Compression has nothing to do with collection. The use of false technique is the reason

*Dom Giovanni, Lusitano stallion, ridden with a string in his mouth, Sun Valley (PHOTO: MARCIA HART).*

so many trainers are able to school very few horses, only the naturally talented ones for the High School.

The job of the *écuyer* is to train ten horses out of ten, and not a few in a lifetime. But most trainers ride only the physical side of the horse, working on his physical difficulties, in an attempt to make those difficulties easier to deal with. No basic mental communication is established.

However, if you start to compress, you escalate the difficulties that exist as well as create physical fear in the horse. But few trainers take the responsibility for this. The horse is accused of being unlevel and unable to produce collection. Compression is responsible for this inability. Can you imagine a ballet dancer bound with rope, then whipped and spurred in order to make him perform beautifully?

I'm sure you have heard the expression "driving" aids. Leave that word for people sitting behind carriage horses. We must allow the horse to perform, allow him to enjoy his job, not drive him.

Any contact more than the weight of the reins will destroy lightness and the horse's cooperation in performing; it will force the horse to respond with resistance. Any contact that does not allow for lightness of the horse's lower jaw contracts the whole horse and makes any kind of true collection impossible. It produces compression, making the engagement of the hindquarters difficult or impossible.

How can the novice trainer tell when his horse is truly light? The horse must be going forward and on the bit. Then the only contact with the horse's mouth is the weight of the rein leather, in impulsion. If the horse's frame is contracted, and the horse isn't going anywhere, you have a false frame.

# 12

## Lightness versus Contact

Baucher used to say, "Every horse has the same mouth." Of course, everyone laughed at that, because they knew there was a soft mouth and a hard mouth. (A "hard mouth" refers to a horse so stressed and tense in his body that the rider feels all the resistance in his mouth. A "soft mouth" refers to a horse that is fairly supple and comfortable in his mind and body, and you feel the lack of resistance in his mouth.) What he was trying to say, however, was that every horse was capable of being light if put into the proper balance.

The important thing to understand is that, in a state of lightness, the horse can overcome most of his problems of balance and conformation. If the horse is not balanced, he feels restricted, rigid. You must know what the correct balance is, put the horse there, then wait and leave him alone. This relationship between balance and lightness is why the rider must have a constant obsession with the latter.

When there is contact with the mouth more than the weight of the rein, it is impossible for the horse to have a relaxed back. There is resistance starting from the jaw and traveling all the way down the spine; the horse contracts himself all over, especially in the part that created the problem in the first place.

There are different levels of lightness during the training of the horse. At the beginning, some *rare* young horses need what I will call "the green horse contact," which is a shorter rein and more contact, since they have to learn to keep their bodies together. Then, when the horse is forward and together, you can work on lightness.

A horse's habit of getting strong in his mouth can be created by two things. First, it can be caused by a lack of balance. He is using your hands to balance himself. Secondly, the horse can have a mental problem about wanting to hang onto your hands or resist, in which case you must go back to longeing and work in hand to regain his complicity.

## THE BEHIND-THE-BIT
## CONTROVERSY

Another familiar controversy is that of on-the-bit versus behind-the-bit. This is often what happens when you ask a young horse that has been in the field for three years to work in the on-the-bit position. A good deal of mental and physical change must happen first. Physically, most of the young horses are not capable of staying on the bit, and have a tendency to roll in their heads or overbend, because of a lack of muscle on the top line. If you make sure in these cases that the side reins are long enough and that the horse has plenty of impulsion, this will be a temporary problem until the horse builds the proper muscle.

The only real danger in overbending is when the horse is

afraid of the hand of the rider; he is on the bit through the abusive use of the hand. Once this situation is established, it is very difficult for the horse to trust and have confidence again. If this is the case, you basically need to do the work in hand again with the horse in the correct position until he understands he is not to be afraid of the rider or the hand. And, of course, you make sure he is truly forward on the longe line. That should do it. The reward is a pat or stopping work immediately. (Also, as a reward or between sessions of work, you can let the horse go long to relax him, but I don't work all of them that way systematically.)

The real danger lies in not having the horse behind the bit, but behind the leg. This is an old expression that means he is not forward in his mind, and it is one of the worst problems that you can have. These two things should not be confused.

## THE NONHALF HALT

The idea of the half halt, which riders use to constantly correct the horse, is wrong on two levels.

First of all, as we have already determined, we do not want to correct the horse all the time but to educate him as to the balance we want and allow him to maintain it. The second misconception about the half halt is the belief that physically, and only physically, a man is capable of rebalancing 1,200 pounds of horse that does not have a mind. This is what the half halt purports to do.

We all agree on the desirability of harmony between horse and rider. I'm not sure that the horse enjoys those half halts, or that they can create any kind of harmony.

So here we find ourselves faced with two very different and conflicting approaches: according to one, the rider considers his horse wrong and unbalanced and spends the rest of his life trying to fix it through a series of half halts; according to the other, the rider believes he can create the original balance, meaning the best that the horse is able to produce at that time, and try to maintain it. In other words, the second approach does not believe in constant correction from the rider. Those who use it believe in letting the horse educate himself through a progression of movements that make the horse himself more aware of his own balance. That is what I believe to be the definition of self-carriage.

What does one do to rebalance the horse when he loses his balance? First, ask yourself why the horse lost his balance. You can then use a series of techniques to make the horse aware of his unbalanced state and suggest that he correct it. For example, one can use movements such as shoulder-in and haunches-in in different directions from a straight line to a circle and back to a straight line, concentrating on recreating the original balance that we had before we started the movement.

And of course, the proper use of the upper part of the body of the rider in connection with different lengths of the rein will help. When the upper part of the rider's body goes slightly back, his hands will go slightly up, and this will act upon the horse by the same principle as the fulcrum of an antique scale (see the figure on page 87). When the fulcrum goes back, then the front of the horse will be elevated and the horse will sit on his haunches. There are different degrees of this.

The use of the half halt as the preparation for a movement is completely unnecessary because you may contract the whole horse. One commonly hears instructors say, "Before you do such and such, do a half halt." The half halt is supposed to mean, "Hello, do you want to do something?" I don't think the equivalent of a kick in the teeth is needed for that.

When the horse has no contact in his mouth with the reins, he can relax his back all the way through the spine. That makes a half halt useless; there is nothing to rebalance from because the horse is relaxed and balanced.

When the horse is rigid and his jaw is locked, the use of the half halt makes the rider look as though he is rebalancing a piece of wood and making the horse more rigid in the process. That kind of rigidity is mostly shown in the lack of correct work from

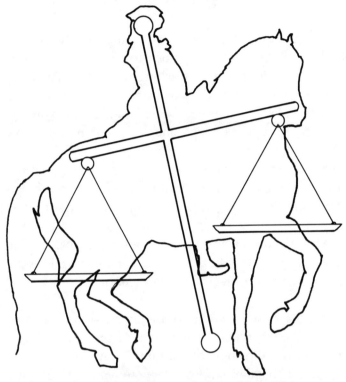

*The antique scale and its analogy to body position. The upper part of your body acts like a fulcrum to make the horse "sit" on his haunches.*

the hindquarters. The horse is not able to give his maximum. It shows up in the inability to lengthen the walk because the horse is contracted. It shows in the artificial lengthening at the trot; the horse "shoots at the moon" with his front legs. The horse looks as though he is doing a low Spanish trot in coordination with a dragging back end. This has nothing to do with a real lengthening, in which a horse relaxes and has the same movement in the front as well as the back.

The constant contact and the half halt are also responsible for the loss of rhythm in the pirouette at the walk and canter, and for the absence of true *piaffer* and *passage,* because relaxation is missing.

## THE REIN BACK

A lot of riders are concerned with teaching their horses the rein back. I basically never teach my horse to rein back. Either he does it or he doesn't do it, but no teaching is involved. As we said in chapter 5, the horse should be aware enough of his body that he can rein back. When the rider is seated on him, it is a question of his back being strong enough and round enough to allow the rein back to happen.

The stronger the back of the horse, the more he can allow you to sit on him and lean back. If the horse has a weak back, sit on him as lightly as you can to allow that weak back to round up under you.

The visualization of a slow-moving tennis ball hitting the wall and returning to you is a correct one for the rein back, and helps the rider to understand the short amount of time the hand is used.

First, make sure you do not lose impulsion when you halt. Then, a very short, timed closing of the fingers will act like a wall and reverse the direction of the impulsion. Ask for very few strides at the beginning. Be happy sometimes with just the thought. If the horse understands, that's the most important thing.

In training the horse, you have to mentally separate the rein back from the *piaffer* and the *levade*. Each has a very distinct balance, and they should never be confused. For people who ride only physically, the aids for all three are the same, just as the aids for the canter depart and the half pass are physically the same.

# 13

# *Working Systematically*

## HOW TO PRACTICALLY
## APPLY MY SYSTEM

Dressage is systematic training. The training of a horse is most effective when it is applied as a system. However, there is a difference between systematic work and routine work. I do not believe in routine work that destroys spontaneity and makes the horse into a machine.

Instead, I believe in what I call "instant quit." That means that if a horse does something well, I reward him instantly by stopping the work. I would never plan to do, say, twenty continuous minutes of work at the trot. If the horse does what I ask, I stop. In order to improve, a horse must be willing to do his best for you, and the great trainers have always known when the horse has done this and reward him for it.

Of course, his best doesn't mean perfection. It just means the best that particular horse can do in that particular movement, on that particular day of his life. But if you do not recognize the horse's best effort when he produces it, and ask him instead to repeat the movement by rote, he will learn to do that rather than give you 100 percent of what he can do. The horse learns that he had better conserve his energy for doing what you ask over and over again. Thus he will learn to give you a 30-percent effort instead of his best.

The system that I use to begin work is as follows (assuming that the horse already has been longed and worked in hand):

First, the rider must be in the correct position. You must sit as far forward in the saddle as possible. You must sit lightly and learn to feel the vertical position. To position the upper part of the body, imagine that someone is pulling a hair on the top of your head back and up. The shoulders should be relaxed, back, and down. Finally, elbows should be at your side, hands resting lightly on the front of the saddle so that they do not move.

Most riders do not understand the concept of the fixed hand, which is the basis of lightness. It is a rare horse that will pull against a truly fixed hand. Horses are not that stupid. They pull against hands that move. And many more people think that they can keep their hands from moving than can actually do so.

One often hears the misguided expression, "The horse is leaning or pulling on the hands." The best way I have to illustrate that misconception is to have the rider hold a longe line, while I hold his other hand. I ask the rider to pull, acting like the horse. As soon as he does so, I give unconditionally to him by opening the fingers and dropping the contact, showing how impossible it is to pull when nobody is pulling back.

In the same way, one cannot lean against nothing. One needs a wall or contact to lean against. The concept of lightness comes from the fact that your hand, by the quick opening and closing of the fingers, does not allow the horse the opportunity to pull or lean.

The best way to make sure your hands do not move is to put them on the front of the saddle. You can tie a string on the front of your saddle (looping it through the breastplate dee) and place your little finger under the string. This does not prevent you from using your fingers. You can still open and close them, but you cannot begin a tug of war with your horse.

If the rider's position is correct, it is time to adjust the reins. The correct length of rein depends on what you want to do, on the conformation of both horse and rider, and on the training of the horse.

The reins must always be the right length to allow the horse to be on the bit. If the horse is not on the bit, then what you are doing is not dressage.

As I mentioned briefly in chapter 12, I find that it is often necessary to start with a rein that is "too short" in order to have the untrained horse on the bit, especially short-coupled horses like Arabs. These horses have a tendency to be a little more difficult than average to convince that being on the bit is good for them. They do not allow compromise. You have to ask for 150 percent from them in order to have a safety margin. My expression is that the reins "allow the horse to stay in a good position." Later the reins will be longer, but at the beginning the "too short" rein is, in fact, the correct length.

Make sure the horse is on the bit at the halt. The halt has a basic advantage: Since you are not in motion, it is easier for both the horse and rider to think about what they are doing. Put the horse on the bit at a square halt. Close the leg and maintain the light leg pressure, if necessary. Keeping the hands on the saddle, close the fingers. Lean back with the upper part of the body.

Then try this at the walk. If the horse loses the position of on the bit, halt. Put your hands on the saddle. Check your body to make sure it is in the correct position. Make sure you have a correct length of rein. If the horse loses impulsion in the walk, first think more clearly. Project your mind. Know where you want to go. Then relax your body. Use the leg lightly again. Then touch the horse with the whip. Always communicate with the horse in this order: think, relax, use the leg lightly, and then the whip. Always play with the fingers to have the horse light. Most people cannot work at the walk because their horses are not light.

You must make a green horse understand what playing with the fingers means until it is easy for him. If he begins to pull or lean, drop the contact by a quick forward movement with the inside hand. Then reposition the hand on the saddle. Be sure not to pull yourself, and if you feel the horse start to pull, drop the contact. Do this with alternate hands.

You can do this with the rhythm or against the rhythm of the gait, with the movement or against the movement. Timing is important. If it does not work, if the horse is not on the bit and light, then the timing is wrong. Keep a consistent attitude and wait.

If nothing happens, reposition your hands and develop a feeling of more impulsion, first with your mind, using whatever imagery works for you, such as warming up your gorgeous Ferrari in your driveway before taking it out on the road. Then ask lightly with your legs. If the horse is still not on the bit, you must proceed to using Baucher's flexions in hand, as follows.

Baucher's flexions are helpful in that, by overflexing the horse laterally, they convince the horse that he can bend his neck excessively without losing his balance. They convince him that he can do it mentally as well as physically. During these flexions, make sure that the horse is as square as possible, or at least that the inside hind leg is as much underneath the horse as possible. The goal is to have a relaxed lower jaw with the head up and as vertical as it can be. The trainer will be conscious of the importance of the interrelationship between the bending toward the inside and the stretching of the outside of the neck. When the horse is on the bit, give with the fingers immediately to allow the lower jaw to relax.

You must know what you want to do, where you want to go, and how you want to go. Unless you are certain about these things, it will be difficult to go on to the next step, which is to project your mind in the desired direction. You want to maintain relaxation and lightness while you ask for impulsion. Loosen your back. Think forward. Think the rhythm that you want. Ask politely for it with a light pressure of your legs, if necessary.

Remember that relaxation is essential. If the movement is done with any tension, it cannot possibly have the effect of suppling the horse. This means that you use only the minimum pressure of your legs necessary to get the effect that you want. If he does not respond as you wish, touch him with the whip. But before you do, close the fingers, which are still resting on the saddle, on the reins. Put your upper body back and sit lightly. It's usually easiest to establish the position at the halt, then proceed to the walk, closing the fingers on one rein, and then the other, to maintain lightness.

Sometimes, but rarely, the trot will be easier, but the advantage of the walk, as I have said before, is that both horse and rider think better the slower they go. You need to establish a slow, controlled, active walk with a clear four-beat rhythm. Go on a circle on the horse's easier side—usually this will be the left. (Why is this so? I don't know. That is the way they are, possibly due to the position in the womb. I just know I see more horses whose easy side is the left rather than the right, just as one meets more right-handed people than left-handed ones.)

If the walk is not correct, halt and reestablish better communication between horse and rider. It often helps to walk six strides and halt, then repeat: exactly six strides and halt. This is a good test of control. Each time you halt or walk, do less. Your goal is to establish mental communication with the horse. Do less to obtain more. You should begin go have the feeling that he hears you think "halt" or "walk on."

With a trained horse, this work has been accomplished almost immediately after the rider mounts. The trained horse is relaxed, attentive, and on the bit immediately. But with an untrained horse, a variety of problems may develop, and it may take days or even weeks of work to get as far as the circle left in a slow, active walk on the bit.

## THINK TO MAKE
## TRAINING NONROUTINE

The rider must always be thinking twenty strides ahead of where he or she actually is. Project your mind as you did when, to turn left, you looked left.

Mental attitude is predominant over a physical aid, as when, for example, the horse is falling in on the circle. The real problem is that the horse is not really forward, and that the direction is not given properly by the rider. Think about a larger circle, a much larger one that extends outside the ring. Your thinking becomes an exaggeration of what you want. Project your mind beyond the wall. Think about shoulder-in if necessary. It makes the horse loosen the shoulder, if there is a problem with it. Make sure your physical position will allow the mental communication. The inside leg must be lightly in contact to allow the horse to bend. (Hands and legs are effective by position, not by action.)

If the horse is falling out, think about a smaller circle. Use the outside aids (legs and a quick touch with the whip on the outside). Your outside hand can be higher, with a slight closing of the fingers. If this does not work, reinforce your thinking, and try vibrating the outside hand. If he puts his haunches out, make sure your outside leg is slightly back and in contact.

To check how effective your mental communication with the horse is, decide to stop at a certain point along the wall, such as the mirror. Project your mind to stop at this point well before you are there. Then, six strides before the halt, lean back, sit lightly, straighten your back, become taller. Your lower leg, like the hand of a good dancer, must be on the horse to provide mental and physical support for the halt.

Play with the fingers to ask the horse to put his nose down. In fact, before any transition up or down, you should play with the fingers to ask him to put his nose down, since he must be especially correct before you ask for anything. As soon as you feel the horse is ready, ask for the transition. If nothing happens, ask again with more emphasis and a light closing of the fingers.

If he still doesn't stop, analyze the problem. Is it a problem of communication? Does he understand what you want? Or is it a problem of impulsion? Is he asleep? Or is it a problem of balance? If he doesn't understand what you want, explain again. If he is asleep, reestablish the activity of your walk. If it is a problem of balance, go back to shoulder-in.

When the horse does stop, ease the hands and relax your

body and your mind. Your goal at the halt is *"descente de main et descente de jambe,"* the ceasing of all aids. Stop for a count of eight. Every time you stop you have a fantastic opportunity to start all over again with a new horse and a new rider.

When you have a good walk, you are ready to trot. Be clear where you want to go. Be extra relaxed. Pay extra attention to the hands, which are on the saddle and do not move. Shorten the reins. Decide which trot you want, of the hundred possible ones there are. If you want a walk in preparation for lengthening, it is going to be very different than a walk in preparation for *piaffer*, just as a trot before an extension is very different than a trot before *piaffer*. Decide which rhythm and which attitude (of collection) you want. You must build impulsion before you begin the movement. With a green horse, you want a minimum of impulsion in order to have a maximum of relaxation.

Ask for the trot first by thinking about a trot, then by loosening your back. Have the seat and back ready to go with the horse. Use your leg lightly, and your voice or the whip if necessary.

Mentally check the work at the trot. First, direction: You must be looking where you are going. Second, is the rhythm correct? Every horse has a rhythm in which he is most comfortable. Third, is the horse bent in the direction in which he's going? Fourth, is he light?

When you have a good trot, you are ready to canter. The procedure is the same as for the walk or trot. Look, project your mind. Be clear about what rhythm you want. Start on a circle on the horse's easy side. Build impulsion before you ask for the transition.

Check your position. Your outside hand should be higher in order to place the horse on his haunches. Your outside shoulder should be back. Your outside leg is back, slightly behind the girth.

Check the position of the horse. He should be bent to the inside. The degree depends on the conformation of your particular horse, but usually, less bend is better. In general, the bend is proportional to the length and thickness of the neck of the horse.

Long and thin necks will not take as much bend as thick, short necks.

If the horse is ready, ask him to canter, first by visualization. Then use a quick touch with your outside leg, like the tap of a whip, and then relax. Do not compress the horse with a lot of tension in your leg. If he does not respond, you must build impulsion with the mental message first, the voice second, then the whip to reinforce the image.

In the canter, it is important to maintain the direction in which you are going by looking ahead. Adapt your back to the movement of the horse's back. Your inside knee should go forward with the movement. Think the rhythm. Relax.

Maintain your position by reinforcing your outside leg and keeping your outside hand higher and your outside shoulder back. The horse should be slightly bent in the direction he's going, the same as he would be in the trot.

When the canter is good, start the countercanter, though this may be somewhat acrobatic at first. First, get the horse used to it, and then refine it. Mentally move the wall of the arena and put it on the side opposite the leading leg.

## HORSES ARE TEACHERS

Horses are a rider's best teachers. They tell you how they like to be ridden. This is something a rider should get into his head and never forget.

The art of riding dressage is to have the complicity of your horse. One does this on a practical basis by longeing him on the small circle. You walk, trot, and canter, making sure of the following:

1. He is forward
2. The three gaits are correct
3. He performs those three gaits in a special position

Right at the beginning he has to accept the side reins. Mentally and physically he starts to be with you and then you work him in hand.

Reinforce the forward movement, bombard the horse with visualization. In your head you have which balance and which mental attitude you want from him. When he gives it to you, don't interfere. Disappear, say, "Good Boy," "Bravo," "Fantastic," and then quit.

Day after day, reinforce that mental attitude. Walk, trot, and canter, do the shoulder-in and haunches-in with your horse's brain in tune with yours. Find the original balance, the original rhythm in which he's happy, and the rest of it is only gymnastic.

Horses are simple animals, but they do have brains. They sometimes object when asked to do things they cannot do. They suffer pain. They have accidents when they are young, or they say, "I'm sorry, but I don't want to dance with you." Or they are nice "people," but there is no communication between the horse and rider. If the rider does ask the horse for something, he doesn't ask him precisely enough where to go and what to do.

If riders are good in their thinking, they are sometimes wrong in their bodies. Very few riders are good athletes and have natural balance. We all compensate for our own physical difficulties. That comes after retraining your mind through visualization exercises, which I talked about earlier.

Some riders have the gift of nonintervention, as I mentioned before. That's what makes a gifted rider. He gets a clear picture of what he wants in his head. He has a perfect understanding and does not interfere. It is so clear it is like a detailed painting. The picture even includes emotions, how he is going to feel in that movement.

This can be done consciously. Merely project yourself in time and space ahead of you with a precise vision, projecting a certain rhythm.

Horses do pick up on riders' visualizations, as anyone who has been in trouble or in mental or physical distress can attest. I believe horses give you pictures too, when your mind is open and free enough to receive them. I believe that is the way they communicate with each other as well.

## HORSES WITH PROBLEMS

Most problems come from spoiled horses who have been abused. With them one must use more mental domination with longeing and work in hand in order to have the horse trust man once again. Then one has to estimate which part of his problem is mental and which part is physical, which positions or movements the horse associates with pain or discomfort or with flashbacks that mean, for him, discomfort or pain.

A horse can be mentally lame, meaning that he is not using one leg or his back properly because of an early accident or injury. The part that was hurt sent a message to the brain: "I'm hurt, protect me." The brain then sent the message back to the leg saying, "Protect yourself, and you will heal." Over a long period of time the latter message stayed as an image in the horse's brain, constantly present, even after the original cause of the pain message was gone. After we have established basic mental communication with that horse, we have to interfere with his brain to send a new message: "You are healed, try to use that leg again." That way we begin the process of reeducation.

In order to establish quality communication between you and the horse quickly and successfully, your own mental attitude is very important. An open, analytical, positive attitude is necessary; no bad feelings and no anger, no matter what happens, which means discipline and self-restraint. Then you must have the knowledge of where you have to position your body in order to establish real communication regarding what you want from the horse.

Following are a few of the more common horse problems I see:

- Some horses seem made of gelatin; their spines won't stay straight, and riders cannot get them together. Once one thing is adjusted, something else, a shoulder or a leg, falls out. This is very typical of young horses, which seem made of rubber. Generally speaking, this rubbery feeling can be a real problem. It becomes a difficulty for most riders, because the more they try to establish a contact, the worse the rubbery feeling gets. The latter is caused by lack of forward movement combined with a lack of muscle in the horse. To correct it, go to a really forward gait, sometimes even one that is a little too fast, using speed as a substitute for straightness. Picture the horse's spine as part of an enormous straight line in the direction you are going. Do a lot of up- and downhill riding outside. This will make the horse more forward in his brain and help build his muscles. Try not to pressure the horse by establishing the kind of contact that will create a problem.

- Sometimes the horse will go down on the bit for a few strides, then come up again. When the rider gets him back down, he stays there for a few strides, then comes back up again. Something is obviously bothering him. Maybe his balance is not quite right. Once again, we assume longeing and work in hand has been done correctly, and the horse is physically able to keep the position. Perhaps the rider is getting tense, his hands are moving, or the rein is too long and he is unable to keep the horse light.

- The horse that gets pacey at the walk is a tough one. The lack of purity of the gaits is a serious problem. First, look into why the horse is nervous. Is it a matter of diet? Eliminate oats, sugar, or alfalfa if they are suspected of causing the problem. If the horse is strong by nature, coordinate a series of longeing and work-in-hand sessions to make him as relaxed as possible. When you walk, do a lot of halts, and then walk some more.

- What about the horse that takes the reins from the rider and pulls? Or jerks the reins out of the rider's hands? We go back to the rider respecting the horse's mouth and the horse the rider's hand. The horse has to be told he must respect the hand just like the little kid that steps on your toes. Generally, the horse that is longed in side reins will stop doing that. You can reinforce this respect during work in hand with a vibration in the rein to say no. When the rider is in the saddle, putting the hands on the front of the saddle will make the horse realize that the reins are like side reins.

- There may be many reasons why the horse won't give his back to the rider at the beginning of a ride or lesson. For one, the horse may not be not supple enough. If the horse is capable of suppleness, he may merely have a temporary problem of tension. Maybe the rider is doing too much. This should not happen if the horse has been longed first with side reins. Perhaps you jumped too fast from the longe line to the saddle. Mentally, go back to your visualization of the relaxed horse.

- If the horse fears a particular spot, such as *X* or an open door in the ring, and spooks repeatedly, it is due to a lack of mental communication between the horse and rider. Fear in the horse shows a lack of positive reinforcement from the rider. It is associated with a rigid body on the part of the horse. The horse is tense, then looks for an excuse to spook or shy. This problem also may indicate a lack of relaxation on the part of the rider. Mentally, go around the field and "listen to the birds," then visualize strongly what you want to do.

## SOME RIDER POSITION PROBLEMS

If the rider is stiff in the back, and tilts the pelvis forward, I make him sit in a chair position in the saddle, with both legs in front of the saddle on the horse's shoulders until he can feel both seat bones. Then I ask him to put his legs back without changing the angle of the pelvis. In that position, the rider can lean back a little behind the vertical, allowing his lower back to follow the horse. It also prevents him from gripping with the knee. I have him make sure his stirrups have only the weight of his toes in them and that his legs are as relaxed as possible.

A rider's stiffness in the shoulders and upper body is a result of too much intellectual thinking or fear. I have the rider make little circles with the shoulders back and down in order for him to feel their stiffness, and I ask him to tell me, while he rides, the story of the last movie he saw, or the plot of the last book he read. Suddenly the problem disappears.

Some riders are unbalanced and sit with one shoulder or hip collapsed. All lack of balance or squareness in the rider is generally a compensation for lack of thinking. The rider believes one shoulder or leg or seat bone is going to do the trick. He puts more weight on one leg and then the body will shift. In order to correct this, the rider has to change his mental attitude. The instructor has to make him relax, smile, and understand that the less he does, the more the horse will do. To help the rider visualize this, I put the horse in a position such as shoulder-in and let the rider feel what it is like to do nothing while the horse does the movement.

Another common problem is the rider who tips his head down continuously and looks at the horse's neck as he rides. Imagine how disastrous it would be to drive your car while looking down at the steering wheel. The rider should train himself to ride as if driving his car, looking ahead where he is going. Send your mind ahead of you. Visualize yourself riding your horse on the track or road ten or twenty strides ahead of you.

However, and I repeat myself again, whatever physical difficulties the rider may find he or she has, it is his or her mental attitude that is far more important. A good, positive mental attitude can overcome a lot of physical problems.

To confirm and illustrate this, let me tell you of a student I have in Hawaii who has severe physical disabilities. She has a pronounced lateral curvature of her spine, which is also fused, and one of her legs is shorter than the other. But, because of her superb mental control and ability to center herself, she is able to produce a very equal shoulder-in right and left.

*Part III*

# THE
# MOVEMENTS

# 14

# The Basic
# Gaits and the Goals
# of Dressage

## THE WALK

The walk is the most important gait in the training of the horse. It is the gait in which we introduce dressage to the horse, establish basic communication with him, and ask him to be conscious of the placement of his own feet. It is also at the walk that we introduce the shoulder-in and all the other lateral movements.

The French have a saying about the walk, that it is *"certainement l'allure la plus marquante dans le dressage du cheval,"* which translates, [the walk is] "certainly the most influential gait in the training of the horse."

The walk, more than any other gait, must come from the horse, and the rider can rarely create it. Therefore, the rider must allow the horse complete mental and physical freedom. The only important thing that the rider has to do at the walk, if the horse is on the bit, is to look where he wants to go, think about the rhythm, keep a light bend even on the straight in the direction in which he is going, and maintain a consistent lightness, which is very important.

Cadence, or a quality rhythm in the walk, is a consequence of the mobility of the horse in that gait. The more mobility he has, the more cadence he can develop. When the cadence is right, things get easier and you have a flowing feeling. When you walk, you must know precisely the rhythm you want before you start. Try to use as little leg as possible to obtain the walk. In other words, walk by loosening your back and allowing the impulsion to go through. Avoid squeezing and compressing with the leg which will make both horse and rider contract.

Things can go wrong quickly, however, as the walk creates a lot of problems for riders. They don't know what to do with it. They don't feel in control because they don't know the correct footfall. The walk brings on fear of the unknown. A lot of people walk their horses without any idea of the mechanics of the gait. Most riders have a very hard time visualizing the footfall of the walk. They know all the legs move, but it's too fast for them to understand how.

To simplify it, visualize the gait as a three-legged one; this gives you the timing and the feeling of the back legs. The sequence is: one hind leg and then the front leg on the same side, and then the opposite hind leg followed by the front leg on that side. It appears as though the horse's hind leg is pushing the front leg on the same side. When you see one of the horse's shoulders go forward, it happens between the time each one of the two hind legs are being put down on the ground—so when you see the right shoulder go forward, you know that the right hind leg has just touched down and just after that the left hind touches down.

When you are able to feel the timing and movement of the hind legs with your seat, you will be able to know, for example, how big the crossing of the inside leg is in the shoulder-in.

What can go wrong? Practically everything when you walk. The position of the horse may not be good enough. He may not be mentally on the bit enough to keep the position physically when you walk and therefore he will lose balance and rhythm. Stop and do it again. Remember the "blind" Appaloosa exercise for putting horse and rider together (see page 12).

When you walk, a very good way to check the mental communication is to halt. Make the horse stop where you want; picture a cliff right in front of you. To halt, sit lightly, close the fingers, lower legs in contact, stretch upward. Work toward a halt without hands. No tension should be involved in the halt. Make sure the horse's nose stays down.

To go from the halt into the walk, play with your fingers to ask your horse's nose to go lower. One does the same thing before any transition, up or down. Play with the fingers to ask the nose to be extra down, extra correct, slightly more in. As soon as you feel your horse is correct, ask him to walk. Count the number of steps you walk and halt again, each time doing less physically. Lean back, sit lightly.

If you have a problem, then the horse is asleep or doesn't care. Or if the problem is one of balance, go back to shoulder-in, because your horse is unbalanced and on the forehand. When he halts, ease your hand. Look for lightness, relax the body and mind, and go into *descente de main, descente de jambe,* no hands, no legs. You leave him alone. It is a good idea to wait for a count of eight and start again with a "new" horse, "new" rider.

A stiff and nervous horse needs a lot of work at the walk. Keep the walk slow but active. Slowing the walk is in your brain, position, and lower back. The collected walk is slow, elevated, with lots of impulsion. It must be slow enough to allow the maximum lifting-up of the leg.

For knowledge, walk; for rhythm, trot.


## THE TROT

The trot is the easiest gait in which to develop rhythm, but the correct rhythm for each individual horse may be difficult to find. In order to know which rhythm is best, the rider must feel and know the horse's possibilities relative to his conformation. Sometimes rhythm is natural and comes from the horse, and sometimes the horse has no rhythm. In the latter case, the rhythm has to come from the rider.

The rider finds the rhythm that the horse likes at that time and relaxes into it. Most trainers and riders think that going fast for impulsion's sake is great. That is why we have so many horses that are stiff and have no communication with their riders whatsoever. It is difficult to have an important conversation when you are running a sprint around a track.

First, allow the horse to be in a position where he can carry you while he is balanced and on the bit, with a *minimum* of impulsion; balance and rhythm can then exist in a relaxed way. When the horse feels good about it, you have found the rhythm in which the horse is happy.

To begin the trot, the rider has to be extra relaxed in his body. He must pay extra attention to his hands. He must shorten the reins slightly between the walk and the trot. He must decide which trot he wants as far as rhythm and attitude are concerned. Most problems occurring with the trot are due to a lack of impulsion in collection. The rider must build impulsion before the movement begins. Then he has to ask with his mind, loosen his seat, and have his back ready to go with the horse. He can use the voice if necessary.

The seat is the combination of the position of the upper part of your body and the adapted suppleness of your lower back, with the two seat bones sitting in the saddle without moving. The position of the rider's upper body establishes balance in the trot, and the adapted suppleness of your lower back and the physical ability to go with the movement establishes the length of the stride.

That is why there is nothing that you can do with your seat. The seat is not something the rider uses to make the horse do things. The seat allows you to go with the movement of the horse.

Learn the neutral seat to start; no pushing and no driving. Then the horse will adapt his stride to the educated back of the

*Extension in lightness: Dom Francisco, Utah-bred thoroughbred, Sun Valley* (PHOTO: *MARCIA HART*).

rider. When you become a more educated and aware rider, he will listen to your back when you ask for straightness or lengthening at the trot.

For the trot, your visualization is very important. Go for the rounded trot. For more "bubble" at the trot, loosen your back and give with the hands. Keep the trot slow and springy. A fast trot is flat. "More trot" means a longer stride. If the nose comes up at the trot, go back to the walk, or halt and start again, as you went back to the halt in the walk.

Collected trot requires a collected attitude on the part of the rider: shoulders back, spine growing taller, hand generally slightly higher, lower leg back.

For rising trot, keep the same hand position as in sitting trot. Keep playing with the fingers.

## THE CANTER

The quality of the walk and of the lateral work that we do is the foundation for the quality of the canter. Most problems in the canter come from problems in the mechanics of the gait itself. The canter is a succession of three little jumps and then a beat of suspension: one, two, three, up, and then you do it again. One looks for round, elevated steps in a quality canter.

It is important to create the specific canter needed for every movement. You have to decide which kind of canter and what rhythm you want. The basic canter, collected canter, counter-canter, pirouette, flying change, and flying change every stride all require different balances and, sometimes, different rhythms. Your horse must have a different level of canter in his head for each one of these. From a basic canter you can go into a counter-canter, which has a little more collection. You have an even more collected canter for haunches-in at the canter and still more of one for the pirouette. You must know when you put yourself into the position, before you even start a pirouette, that you are going to want a different level of canter.

Just getting into the canter can present problems because most people don't properly prepare impulsion. The horse is not ready if he has a lack of impulsion in his walk or trot.

First the horse has a very quiet gait, a collected trot that is relaxed and light. You know the direction and rhythm you want. The position of the horse is lightly bent with no resistance to the inside rein. Your inside hand is higher, your body is back, your outside leg is back, you have the balance and the impulsion, and you say, "Now."

It is as if you are having a short conversation with your horse in which you ask, "Are you ready?" When the horse replies, "For what?" you say, "Canter." He says, "When?" "Now," you say.

The canter depart is an "up" feeling. You imagine the horse climbing into his canter. You must ask for the canter depart with a whisper; always ask for it mentally first, then with a click of the tongue and a bit of your outside leg if it is needed. It is very important that your outside leg is loose and that your inside rein is light. Your leg should act by its position and by the difference of pressure from a relaxed leg. The excessive use of the leg, as I have said before, contracts the horse. That's why I don't like it. Your leg should be as passive as possible but in light contact with the horse, like the hand of a good dancer. It is a mental support more than anything else.

The canter is a gait in which the inside lateral pair of legs of the horse is always in front of the outside lateral pair. In order to be "with" this gait, put your inside leg forward, your outside leg back, and feel your inside knee going slightly forward over his leading leg.

The rider's body is passive during the canter. Look where you want to go on the circle, sit lightly, following the horse with your lower back, your inside knee going forward as the horse's shoulder goes forward. Your inside shoulder is also slightly forward as the horse's same shoulder goes forward; the angle of the rider's shoulder is parallel to the angle of the horse's shoulder.

Always, in the canter, have slightly more contact on the outside rein than the inside rein in order to maintain the horse's balance. Always do your transitions on the outside rein in order to allow the inside leg of the horse to come underneath him.

Pay a lot of attention to the first five strides; that's what determines the ongoing quality of the canter. The rhythm should be slow, slow, slow. If you are not pleased with the quality of the canter, if the horse does not feel round and light, stop and do it again.

Do not let the horse become dependent upon you to keep him going in the canter. The rider's mind perpetuates the canter, not his body. I do not advise people to canter on and on for a long period of time. A few circles of the ring is enough if all is going well.

To do a small circle at the canter, your outside hand is slightly higher than your inside hand, with slightly more contact, your outside leg is back, the rhythm is slow. Slow down the canter with your mind and with your outside hand higher and your fingers closing in rhythm; when your horse is up, close.

The canter is rarely used in early training to improve the horse. One of the most popular misconceptions is that every young horse has a disastrous, or greatly unbalanced, canter. Some have a naturally balanced one. But once in a while you will find a young horse that has an okay walk, a bad trot, and an even worse canter. Most young horses, if correctly worked at the walk and trot, will canter correctly too. The power of the rider's mind can greatly help accomplish this. I use what I call the concept of "painting your horse gray," or changing his color.

I used to have two horses, one a young bay and the other an older, trained gray. After the basics were done with my young horse I still had difficulties with his canter. While I was riding the young horse I visualized so strongly I convinced myself I was riding the old gray, feeling his canter, expecting it, experiencing it. Mentally, I was riding my gray horse. In one day, the canter of my young bay horse improved 80 percent because I expected it to be good. That's a good story and a true one.

# 15

# Transitions in
# General

The gift of noninterference is invaluable for the quality of transitions more than in anything else in riding. The rider must try to be *with* the horse, keeping his own body from interfering with the horse's as much as possible.

One should really not have to work physically on transitions. A transition, as the word indicates, is just a passing moment between two good, balanced gaits. Make the gaits quality ones and there will be good transitions in between. If the horse is balanced before the transition, then the transition will be correct.

Transitions should be educated; you must know and visualize exactly what your next gait is going to be and what rhythm, degree of impulsion, length of stride, and attitude of collection you need before the transition.

Before a transition, make sure the horse is extra correct, ask that his head be a little lower. Keep the same head carriage through the transitions up and down. Play with the fingers through the transitions, but do not move the hands during them.

When you achieve this readiness, ask for the transition mentally, in relaxation, with no tenseness. Make sure both your horse's and your own mental and physical attitudes are correct. The rider should be relaxed and his position correct, shoulders back, for transitions. The horse is relaxed but attentive, on the bit and light. Breathing correctly, in tune with the horse's breathing, is especially important for relaxation. The rider seeks the best quality gait. Impulsion is created before the movement. The rider plays with the fingers for correctness, then visualizes what he wants, then straightens the back for a downward transition, or loosens it for an upward one.

For transitions upward, extra relaxation and giving of the rider's back is necessary to allow the back of the horse to adapt to the new movement. Any strong use of the leg will contract the body of the rider and negate his goal to be one with the horse, and will also make the horse rigid. The wrong rebalancing effect of the hand, meaning the half halt, will do the same thing. (See page 85 on the nonhalf halt.)

Transitions downward are the same, except that the back of the rider straightens, as if one hair on the top of his head was being pulled up and back. He must pay extreme attention to following the back of the horse with his back. The rider's lower leg is lightly on the horse for mental and physical support.

Shortening of the reins between the walk and the trot is necessary in the early stages of training. Transitions downward from canter to trot are done with the support of the outside rein only, so that the inside shoulder does not fall in. Make sure the inside rein is light so that it does not counteract or stop the inside hind leg from working and having a balancing effect.

Exaggerating the situation in your mind is very important in doing transitions with the young horse, especially in the canter-to-trot transitions. One must think "walk," or "halt." The priority in young horses is the quality of the transition over its precision. That will come later. On the bit has priority over the movement itself, and lightness is the overall goal.

When something goes wrong and you ask for the transition and nothing happens, the problem may be one of communication. The horse is asleep or doesn't care. Reinforce the visual and lightly tap tap with the whip, reopening the dialogue. If it is a problem of balance, then the rider must check the quality of the gait. Stop and begin again.

# 16

## *Les Allongements: Lengthening and Extensions*

Lengthening is an excellent exercise for developing and refining communication between horse and rider. In this movement, more than in any other, the horse has to give you what is desired. The rider's part is actually minimal, basically only to be "with" and following the horse's back.

It is in the extended work that you can really see what kind of training the horse has had. If the horse has been worked in resistance and compression, this will show above all at the lengthened walk. If the horse is compressed, he is not going to change and lengthen his frame, and therefore he will produce a short and hurried step.

Both the lengthening at the trot and the canter can be easily faked. The walk is much more difficult and demonstrates the rider's ability. To lengthen and then extend, create your mental image of what you want to do, visualizing a long stride in the same rhythm. Then create the impulsion and the correct physical position for what you want to do.

It is very important to begin the extension with a certain amount of collection, as much as the rider can get without jeopardizing relaxation. There are a lot of different balances from which the horse can extend himself. The lengthening done from a *piaffer,* for example, is completely different from that done from a shoulder-in. The horse is in more of a sitting position when he starts it out of the *piaffer;* this is a slightly different position than one sees in competition today. It is easier for some horses to do the extension from this sitting position, which is why I like to use it in training.

Set up for yourself goals for the level of collection you want within the limits of the ability of the horse as you know them. When this collection is obtained, then do nothing; stay passive. Most important in the lengthening is a consistent lightness, so the horse stays flexible. Keep your impulsion and lightness, but be sure you do not hold it by force. Collection, as I must repeat again and again because it is so fundamental, comes from the position of the rider, not from compression.

Before you ask, be sure that the horse has the desire to lengthen his frame, lower his head, and make his neck longer. Use no hands, just a playing of the fingers on the reins for lightness. Then put the horse into a longer frame by playing with the fingers, asking his nose to be lower and his neck to be longer. Project your mind where you want to go. Progressively the rider loosens his back so the horse can stretch and move out; he adapts the suppleness of his back to the length of stride that is desired. Be careful not to push the horse; the horse is lengthening, not you. The lower leg is in contact with a light pressure, but it is relaxed. Be sure to project your mental image as the horse lengthens. Be aware of your position through your seat bones. Feel conscious that you are square in the saddle. Give your horse a chance to answer your request and give you some feedback. Ask for very little in the beginning; concentrate on rhythm.

To bring the horse back to you, straighten your back, with the lower leg in contact, and wait. A slight closing of the fingers may help at the beginning; the horse should remain light and on the bit. A discreet use of the voice may be used, but as little as possible.

It is important to realize that the abusive use of the rider's legs for the lengthening produces contraction in the horse and disturbs him more than it helps him. The horse should give his back, the rider allowing the relaxed and loose back of the horse to go up under him. The first steps should be slow and regular. When the horse is ready, decide how many steps you want, four to six strides, remembering never to ask for more than you can take back *in relaxation*. Take your time so that you can achieve regularity of rhythm. This, done at the beginning, will save a lot of time afterwards.

If the lengthening is irregular, give more support on the horse's weaker side with the lower leg and/or the hand. The movement has to be long and low and coming from behind. You should see the horse's back legs pushing and extending. You do not want to see, in front, what resembles a low Spanish trot (the horse extends the leg upward before the leg touches the ground), produced by resistance or compression, too much hand, and a sluggish back end of the horse.

If the horse rushes, he may lose balance. He is not ready; go back to the basics. Or the rider may have a lack of visualization, or is physically abusing the animal. The horse must be comfortable before he will lengthen.

If the rider and horse have trouble with a smooth transition from extension back into collection, that's because the extensions they do are in resistance. Therefore, when the rider wants to go back to collection, he has to use too much of everything, because the horse is out of balance and out of control. Again, never extend more than you can bring back comfortably in relaxation. Put your body in a collected position, your lower leg back, your shoulders back, imagine the feeling of someone pulling one hair atop your head slightly up and back, and use your hands only minimally.

In a training session, it is a good idea to come back to shoulder-in after an extension, in order to soften the horse once again and get rid of all the possible resistance or contraction.

When the horse steps wide behind in the lengthening, it is because the horse is being hurried into collection and being compressed too soon. The front end is not high enough to allow space for the hind legs to step under, so he has to spread the latter. Doing the shoulder-in before the lengthening will create this space as well as produce the correct collection.

The hind leg should be extended as much as the front leg. As the FEI rules prescribe, the toe should be pointed to where the foot is going to land and not higher. When it does point higher, as is seen in competition, it is a result of stress.

# 17

## *Mental Attitude for Collection and Extensions*

T he position of the body of the rider, as we have discussed, is different for different attitudes and for different problems. For a collected trot, the most important thing is that the rider has a collected attitude; you must *think* collection and have a clear goal as to what level of collection you want. At first, ask for little; you must know the limits of your horse.

There is a very strong relationship between the degree of collection you have and the degree of control you have. If the horse has collected himself more than you have asked him to, he is able to use that collection against you and escape your control.

For example, you are sitting on your horse in the arena and doing second-level work. Suddenly a truck passes by the stable and makes a tremendous noise, frightening the horse. When the

*Shoulder-in on silk reins, no bit: Dom Giovanni, Sun Valley* (PHOTO: MARCIA HART).

horse is afraid of something, he collects himself, puts himself in a little ball, and makes himself round, so he can kick out or take off. Even the very young foal does this when he is running free with his mother—he collects himself when he is afraid in order to run away.

In all such situations, when you are working in a certain level of collection and the horse gathers himself and takes off, during the ten seconds that it takes you to shorten the rein enough to where the horse has himself collected, you do not have control.

Your attitude must be at the same level of collection as the horse's, or you are not with him anymore. Listen to the feedback that he gives you through your seat bones. Give your horse a chance to answer your demands.

Collection should come from the position of the rider. Place the hands higher and straighten the spine. Collection has nothing to do with compression. Do not *hold* your horse back. When you obtain the desired level of collection, do nothing except maintain the impulsion and lightness.

In asking for the lengthening of the trot or the extended trot, remember that the essence of this movement is that the horse should maintain his balance and his roundness, lengthen his neck, and give his back.

In order to check to see if the horse is ready to lengthen, play with the fingers. Is he light? If so, loosen your back as much as you want the back of the horse to loosen, then ease the hands. Think of the rhythm you want. If nothing happens, change to shoulder-in to build impulsion. Think about impulsion and collection. Then ask for only five or six strides of lengthening.

If your horse can do five strides, he can do fifty, but it is important to maintain the relaxation. Never ask for more than you can bring back in relaxation. Keep the horse on the bit. To bring the horse back, lean back, sit lightly, keep your lower leg on, and close your fingers slightly. The perfect horse will not need the closing of the fingers.

# 18

## *Understanding the Spirit of the Sideways Movements*

T he sideways movements are performed to improve the quality of the gaits; that is what dressage is all about, improving the
purity and quality of the gaits. These movements are not a goal
in themselves, merely a technique toward improvement.

The many different names for these movements can be con-
fusing: shoulder-in, haunches-in, renvers, travers, two-track, half
pass, head to the wall, tail to the wall, leg yielding. To simplify all
this, we can reduce them all into two movements. First of all, you
have the shoulder-in, which is a very different movement from all
the others. The horse is bent around the inside leg of the rider
and is moving in the opposite direction of his bend. That is, the
horse is bent to the right and is moving to the left in shoulder-in
right, and vice versa for shoulder-in left.

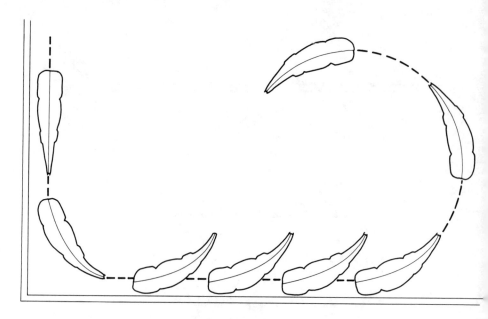

The start and the finish of a shoulder-in on the circle, with the start of the shoulder-in in the corner and then the circle, and then coming out of it.

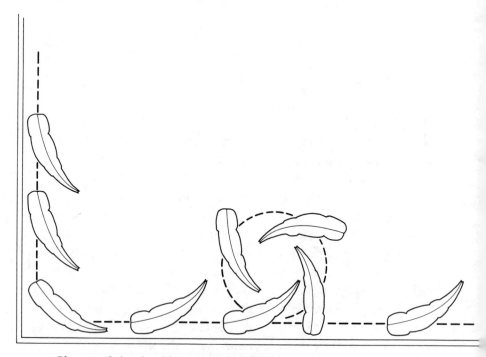

Closeup of the shoulder-in on the circle.

I would call all the other movements a basic haunches-in. The horse bent to the right and moving right is in the haunches-in right. If the haunches-in is done on a diagonal, it is a half pass. If a wall is in front of or behind the horse, it is going to be called something else; that is the only difference among all these other movements. Otherwise the movement is always the same, which is why, to simplify matters, whatever is not a shoulders-in movement will be called haunches-in.

Perhaps it is time to mention leg yielding here and explain why I do not use it. Leg yielding will not be studied here because it is an anticlassical movement and does not have any place in the training of the horse. (The closest thing to leg yielding the French do in training is what we call *pas de côté,* or side pass, which is just like the start of a haunches-in, but with the horse straighter, never counterbent.)

In leg yielding, the horse moves laterally with the horse's head bent in the direction opposite to the movement; the rider's "inside" leg, that is your leg toward which the horse's head is bent, is back, trying to push the hindquarters over. According to the whole of classical thinking, the horse should always be bent around the rider's inside leg at the girth.

Any technique that is going to endanger the goal of allowing the horse to be in balance will make your horse stiff and will not work. That is why leg yielding is so anticlassical, as I have said, because you are obliged to use the inside rein to pull the nose around and bend the horse; the rider is unable to use his inside leg at the girth to bend the horse, because it is back, pushing the hindquarters in the direction in which they are going!

What are the priorities for the sideways movements? Number one in importance is the quality of the gait, which can be defined as follows:

a.  the horse on the bit, relaxed and 100 percent with you
b.  the lightness of the horse, which is proof of the relaxation and roundness of the back.

Number two in importance is the creation of the proper balance for the movement to happen. After the work in hand, the rider should have a pretty good idea of the position and balance needed for the sideways movements. There should be a different degree of position for shoulder-in right and for shoulder-in left, since one direction is always more difficult for the horse. The rider will also have learned the correct position of the horse's head in relation to his back in order to create the maximum use of the back in relaxation. Initially, take care of this area of balance relating to the horse's head carriage, then look for consistency of that balance in that position, and, lastly, try to vary the balance according to the requirements of the different sideways movements.

Number three in importance is the different degrees of collection needed for the sideways movements.

If you have a problem, go back to number one, the quality of the gait, its roundness and lightness. If you still have a problem, check the impulsion, and check the impulsion in collection. *If you lose your bend in haunches-in, go back to your shoulder-in.* From there the horse is going to be on the bit and light again, and produce a quality gait. Then you can go back again to your haunches-in, expecting better quality in that movement.

Sometimes you use a movement just to find and establish a balance and try to keep it afterward, independent of the movement. Sometimes you do just the reverse—you find your balance and you create the movement. Take, for example, the shoulder-in. If your horse finds his balance in the shoulder-in, you should "fade" the shoulder-in and try to keep that balance. With some others, you have to find the balance first and then try to keep it in the shoulder-in.

When introducing the sideways movements to the horse, you must have the minimum of impulsion that will still allow the movement to happen, retaining the maximum of relaxation. You are looking for a mild, relaxed movement from which you are going to increase impulsion while maintaining relaxation. If the horse is tense, he is going to lose it all.

The eventual goal the rider seeks is the optimum mixture of both, the maximum of impulsion with the maximum of relaxation. It goes back to the old classical way of thinking of creating just the necessary energy for the movement—no more, no less.

## SHOULDER-IN

Shoulder-in is a unique movement created by François Robichon de la Gueriniere, who said it was the first and the last movement he taught the horse. He also said every horse has a different degree of shoulder-in, and so it therefore must be adapted as a suppling exercise to the individual horse. It is also a great tool for reestablishing communication between horse and rider when, sometimes, you get into trouble.

Shoulder-in is a movement different from all the others, very fundamental and very dynamic because of its adaptability to different horses. The classical shoulder-in is a four-track movement in order to fully benefit the horse; four tracks make him use his body more. Because it is a suppling exercise, the trainer has to go to the limits of what the horse can do and then carefully ask for a little bit more in order to improve. I use a three-track shoulder-in very little. Most of the time it is useless and of little benefit to the horse, except in the case of one that is chronically rigid, for whom it is a start toward improvement. I always say the three-track shoulder-in is like touching your knee a hundred times. You are not going to get more supple. You need to put your hands on the floor for that, which is the four-track shoulder-in.

The goal of the shoulder-in is to obtain the bend without using the inside rein; the goal of the haunches-in is to do the same thing, with the same bend, with light or no contact on the inside rein. If the horse is in balance, he will be able to do that. As I have explained, any technique such as leg yielding that is going to endanger that goal will make your horse stiff and will not work.

There are different degrees of shoulder-in, as I have also mentioned, but that does not mean you should not go for the real thing. The different degrees of shoulder-in have to do with angles in relation to direction and the different degrees of collection. You are satisfied when you go to the limit of the suppleness of the horse in relaxation and then you ask for a little more. That is why it is an ever-changing movement. As the degree of suppleness in the horse improves and changes, you have to ask for more.

The first day you ride a horse, you can start shoulder-in at the walk, after having done the shoulder-in in the work in hand. During the work in hand, the rider should determine the correct angle for the horse. It is generally different on each side, left and right. How does the rider know the correct angle for four-track? Looking from the front or the back, one should see four legs with the same spacing between them.

Very important in preparation for the shoulder-in is to have a good gait, whether walk or trot, meaning that the horse is on the bit, light and collected. You must have the walk, for instance, in absolute *control* for shoulder-in; have the walk feeling *too* slow. Keep the *same rhythm* from straight walk to shoulder-in and back again. The horse should have nearly the same buoyant feeling in shoulder-in as he has when you want to *piaffer*.

The rider should be able to position the horse into shoulder-in without contracting his leg or body. The way to do that is to consider the positioning of your shoulder-in just like riding a corner or a small circle. Therefore, there is no use of the hand, especially of the inside rein, to position the horse. You imagine that you are beginning a circle and then you will go into shoulder-in. The first step is the most important one because of this positioning; the shoulder-in position is the same position as the first step of the circle.

You position the horse by just looking where you want to go, with your outside rein higher and your inside shoulder back. Your inside leg is positioned slightly forward, the outside leg slightly back. This will allow the horse to give you a few strides of shoulder-in. If you need to do something with your hands, the balance is incorrect or your reins are too long. If done correctly, the shoulder-in enables the inside leg of the horse to be underneath his body. It's the best way to lead the horse into collecting himself. The rider should feel the horse's inside leg swing freer and freer as he goes.

There is a one-two-three timing to beginning the shoulder-in:

1.  the correct positioning of the horse out of the corner
2.  the correct bending of the horse
3.  feeling both horse's shoulders coming in off the track

Then you carry on with the movement.

Do only a few steps and then go forward straight into a circle (see the figures on page 126), that is, with the hind legs on the same track as the forelegs, bent on a circle but no longer in a shoulder-in. Always end shoulder-in this way, with a circle to the center of the arena.

The biggest problem the rider will run into is the tendency to stiffen his body, which will force the horse to go sideways. As a result, horse and rider are not going forward anymore. The horse answers the stiffness of the rider with the stiffness of his own body.

If the horse goes through your hands, that is, does not respect direction, you have to stop and try again. First, create a better balance and then repeat the movement. It is always better to do the movement again correctly from the start than to correct it as you go.

If there is too much bend in the neck in shoulder-in, check the inside rein to see if it is light and then raise the outside rein slightly. If the horse runs into or falls into shoulder-in, lighten the inside hand.

Shoulder-in in preparation for lengthening will be different from a shoulder-in in preparation for *piaffer*, as far as balance is concerned. A more "sitting," more collected shoulder-in is needed to prepare for a *piaffer*. (To lengthen from the shoulder-in, put the outside leg on, give with your hands, and loosen your back.)

Always return to the shoulder-in to relax and then go on to a long rein, loose rein. If the horse cannot stretch, that means he has some back problems and you need more work at the shoulder-in to help remedy them.

The shoulder-in is one of the most difficult movements to do correctly, but when done well it is the key or solution to unlocking a lot of problems and allows the horse to feel and be free.

## HAUNCHES-IN

The same continuity of movement that we have tried to maintain in longeing, work in hand, and riding should exist with shoulder-in, haunches-in and the pirouette.

For the haunches-in, the rider's position never changes in relation to the horse; only his position in relation to the direction changes. To do a haunches-in, have your outside hand high, your outside shoulder back and your outside leg back. The less leg used, the better. The goal is to have a light inside rein and have the horse as light as possible. If you get stuck, it is because the horse lacks forward movement, so go forward and straight and, after upgrading impulsion in collection, try it again.

The rider's shoulders should be parallel with the horse's shoulders in haunches-in, just as in shoulder-in (see the figure on page 133). Lean way back in collection position for both; it is your mind that tells the horse to go forward.

Haunches-in is basically the same at the trot as at the walk. Be careful of the rhythm and be happy when you get a few strides, always knowing that the horse has to stay on the bit and be relaxed. There's no chance of doing it with a stiff, unbalanced horse.

The sense of direction is very important in the haunches-in, as in all the other sideways movements. You have to know where you are going; using a square to do these movements is very important. Doing the sideways movements on a circle is easier for the horse but harder for the rider.

In all the sideways movements, it is important to always be centered. Sit on *both* seatbones, "listening" with them to the

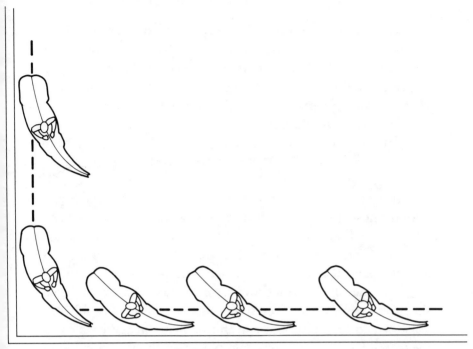

*Shoulder-in to haunches-in, using the corner to go into the haunches-in.*

horse. Going "with" the horse with your lower back is more important than using a strong leg. The less hand and leg one uses to achieve the sideways movements, the better.

## SHOULDER-IN/HAUNCHES-IN

Going from shoulder-in to haunches-in merely requires, as I have said, changing the position of the rider's shoulders. The rider's shoulders are parallel to the horse's shoulders for both shoulder-in and haunches-in. Lean back for both; it is the rider's mind that must tell the horse to go forward.

Concentrate on lightness before, during, and after the transition between these two movements. You can't do anything physical because it is going to upset the horse. A transition should always be done with the horse relaxed.

The complete relaxation of the rider is also necessary. When the horse is in shoulder-in, the only thing you need to do is play with your fingers to work on lightness. The bend in haunches-in will be lost if the shoulder-in preceding it is not full of impulsion. If you should lose the bend in your haunches-in, go back immediately to your shoulder-in.

After shoulder-in/haunches-in, always relax the horse for a short period of time, at any gait, allowing the horse to stretch on the way down.

If the horse is able to walk, trot, and canter on a loose rein with his nose down, it means that your work was done in relaxation. If the horse is unable to do that, it means your work was done in contraction and compression. It is the equivalent of *descente de main et descente de jambe* if he works well this way.

Shoulder-in and haunches-in at the walk and trot are *the* two sideways movements. Everything else is little details. If your horse can do a good shoulder-in and haunches-in at the walk and the trot, he has the basic training to do everything. If something goes wrong elsewhere, then go back to these basic movements. Most of the time you will have overlooked something, such as tenseness in your horse or any other piece of the puzzle, such as the horse not being on the bit, or not going forward, or not having enough collection. Perhaps there is no communication between horse and rider.

## THE PIROUETTE
## AT THE WALK AND CANTER

The most important preparation for doing pirouettes is to have in your mind a clear visualization of the perfect movement before you begin. To do this, you must have a correct knowledge of what a pirouette is: a small circle done in haunches-in, with the inside leg of the horse remaining on the spot but maintaining the mechanics of the gait all the way through.

As a training approach, it is critical for the rider to realize the continuity of thinking between haunches-in and the pirou-

*Pirouette on the long rein: Irish Hill, American thoroughbred* (PHOTO: KATHY CLEAVER).

ette. Mentally speaking, the only difference between the two movements is a change of direction or, actually, of geometry. The progression goes from doing the haunches-in on a straight line to doing the movement on the small circle. Nothing else must change. There must be the same position of the rider in relation to the horse. The change from straight line to small circle does, however, need an upgrade of impulsion in collection, while maintaining lightness.

To begin, first establish the proper gait, which is a collected walk. Then establish proper balance, with the horse as collected as possible, "sitting" on his haunches, but with as much lightness as you can achieve.

With the horse in the collected walk, use the shoulder-in to obtain the correct bend, establishing lightness on the inside rein

*Pirouette at the canter on the long reins: Jeffri, Arabian, Sun Valley* (PHOTO: KATHY CLEAVER).

first, then the outside rein. Get a quality shoulder-in before the pirouette; ask the horse to give a little extra.

Then, with the horse somewhere near the *center* of the ring, go into haunches-in. Have your outside rein a little higher, very slightly to the outside, keeping a light contact. Next, lean back, placing both legs toward the back for more collection, keeping your outside shoulder slightly back; the rider's shoulder should be parallel to the horse's.

Now, look back over your shoulder toward the center of what will be the pirouette, to help visualization. At first, start with a small circle, allowing the back legs of the horse to cross. It is easier for the horse this way, and it is easier for the rider to feel the uninterrupted stepping and crossing of the horse's back legs. You need lots of impulsion, but you must be careful not to use much hand or leg. Don't push with the outside leg; just use it to keep the haunches where you want them. The inside rein is down and passive. Your outside hand is up; lean back with it, but don't pull. You should keep the horse's hips moving and let the horse's shoulders cover the extra ground. Shoulder-in to haunches-in to pirouette must be a building of impulsion in collection; that is more important than the movements themselves. Shoulder-in/haunches-in also leads to *piaffer* and *passage* in the same way.

Next, ask for a smaller circle. If by lack of impulsion or collection (or both) you lose the bend or the haunches-in position, go immediately forward and straight and start the process once again. Once again, have the horse collected, straight, and moving forward. Go back into the shoulder-in and make sure the horse is light on both reins.

The complete passivity and lightness of your inside rein is a must. *Any contact* on it at all, from the horse or the rider, such as to force direction, will be fatal to the correct position of the hindquarters.

When you ask again for the movement, make sure that you have a correct visualization of where the center of the pirouette is. That will help the consistency of the movement.

Be aware of not using your outside leg too much. This error makes a small circle impossible, by moving the horse's haunches too much to the inside.

The rider's lower back must go with the movement as if he were swinging on the seat of a swing. Do not interfere by shifting weight, stiffening, or freezing. The less you do, the more chance your horse will have to perform pirouettes and not be disturbed by your unnecessary gesticulation.

Do not attempt these pirouettes from a position on the wall. This would be too difficult at the start, because of the mental interference presented by the wall. You need to be well in the center of the ring. You can use either the center line or the diagonal; they are equally good.

The more you have mastered the pirouette at the walk, the easier the pirouette at the canter will be. The pirouette at the canter is exactly the same as at the walk. A very collected, sitting-on-the-haunches canter at the start is necessary. Start with the easier lead first. At the canter, lightness will be even more important than it is at the walk. You must be absolutely the lightest you can be for the canter pirouette.

Start with a large circle in haunches-in until you feel the haunches getting lower during one of your strides. Repeat the movement until this feeling becomes more consistent for more strides. When it does, you are ready to ask for the pirouette in exactly the same manner as you did at the walk.

Later, you will be able to start directly into the pirouette from the walk; that is, after one stride of canter forward directly from the walk, having your body well-positioned, you immediately ask for a pirouette. Keeping the rhythm in either gait, but especially at the canter, is extremely important to the outcome of the pirouette.

Since one of the easiest things in the world to do is to get "stuck" at the canter pirouette, to bog down or lose power, mentally visualizing a *double* pirouette helps the correct execution of one. Always finish the pirouette precisely; that is, come out of it exactly where you want to be, on the diagonal or the center line again.

If the horse pivots for the beginning of the pirouette, once again the rider is paying too much attention to the movement and not enough to the gait. The rider wants to do a pirouette too tight, too soon, instead of thinking of a larger circle. A similar thing happens with the haunches-in at the walk. The rider gets rigid and the walk is gone. For me the pirouette is simply a change of direction of a haunches-in at the walk or canter. There's no loss of gait. One still has to think of walking or cantering, and one has to know where the center of the pirouette is.

This problem can also come from the failure of the rider's back to follow the movement. Get tall and lean back with your outside shoulder back, looking toward the inside, and having the feeling of your outside hand going up and out, the elbow always remaining at your side.

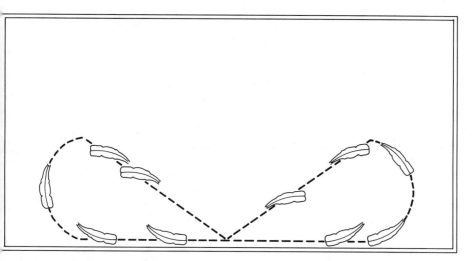

*Shoulder-in left, half-pass left, and then change the bend on the long side of the wall; then you're in shoulder-in right and then back to the wall again. When you meet the track, change the bend again and go into shoulder-in left.*

Having the outside rein slightly higher makes it act as a balancing rein. It controls the outside shoulder during the shoulder-in; it makes the horse sit on his haunches for haunches-in and half passes; it is a great help for pirouette and in the canter work—basically for everything. One always uses the outside rein higher in combination with a very light inside rein. You must be able to have contact on the outside rein when you want it. If you don't want it or need it, that's fine, but if you do need it, you should be able to obtain it at the instant.

## THE HALF PASS

A half pass is basically a haunches-in done on the diagonal without the mental support of the wall. An easy way to start the half pass is from the wall to the quarter line and then half-pass back to the track. The advantage of that is the use of the "magnetic"

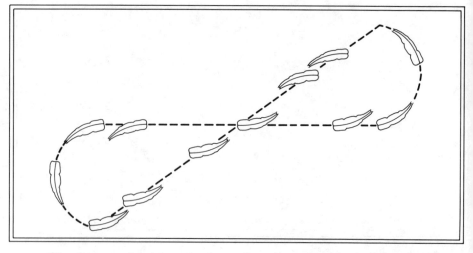

*The diagram involving the center line shows shoulder-in left to half-pass left to shoulder-in left on the center line. That's an exercise you can do when you want to work on a specific bend.*

attraction of the wall. Of course, the disadvantage is that you must straighten and then change your bend before you turn back to the track, and then when you meet the wall you must rebend the horse correctly on that rein. (See the figure on page 139.)

Another technique is to leave the track at the wall and half-pass to the center line, straightening on the center line and proceeding to *A* or *C* where you turn back on the track. In other words, the advantage here is that you don't have to reverse and it allows you to turn in the same direction as the bend and then redo the half pass on the same rein or side. (See the above figure.)

One must understand the importance of having the horse only slightly bent throughout these movements. *Slightly,* once again, means proportional to his conformation. You cannot have a heavy bend as it will work against lightness.

I generally work on the easy side first. I rarely reverse before that side has been suppled and confirmed in the movement. Then I reverse and go through the same process on the other side. I see too many riders not giving enough attention to that concept and reversing without apparent reason, never really working in sufficient depth.

I see too much bend in the neck of most horses in modern competition. There is no real advantage to this and it only succeeds in making the horse look like a contortionist. The amount of bend is dictated by the length and thickness of the neck, as I have said before. The longer and thinner the neck is, the less the amount of bend it should have. The novice rider can tell that the horse is bent too much when the latter stops forward movement, and from the quality of the gait in general.

It is important to maintain light contact with your inside leg to allow the bend. The rider's outside hand is higher to allow the "sitting position" of the horse (see the figure on page 87)—once again, we have the principle of the fulcrum in action. As for the inside rein, the rider must be *obsessed* with its lightness.

If the rider uses too much outside leg, the haunches could lead in the half pass, which is classically incorrect but sometimes useful in training a horse that is basically lazy in his back end. Haunches leading will generally activate the hind end. And it is easier for the horse to go from an exaggerated to a more correct position.

If impulsion is lost, make sure, first of all, that you are relaxed. Any tenseness acts like a brake. Perhaps you did not have enough impulsion in collection to begin with, or perhaps you are asking the horse for too many strides or too much angle. In any case, you are to stop the movement, go straight, and then try it again.

If the horse is balanced in the half pass, the rhythm is there, and if the rhythm is there, everything else will follow. It is important that when the rider meets the wall in half pass he pays attention to the last few strides of the movement. They are the most important strides as far as lightness and rhythm are concerned. Why? Because of the interference of the wall, which tends to have a mental impact. The horse hurries toward the wall and loses both his balance and the bend.

A lot has been written on where the rider should sit during the half pass. One does not sit toward the outside or the inside of the saddle, one sits squarely on it. The rider should be like the little dog in the circus atop the ball. When the ball is in motion, the little dog is moving right along with it. He knows exactly where he should be in order to stay with the movement of the ball.

Canter half passes are generally easier than those at the trot. It is, in fact, more difficult to canter straight than to do canter half passes. At the canter, the rider is going to feel that his weight is going from one seat bone to another because of the movement of the horse. The rider should do nothing with his seat, just make sure he is going *with* the movement.

## COUNTERCHANGE OF HAND

The counterchange of hand consists of the half pass in one direction, one stride of straightening, and then the half pass in the opposite direction. It is very important to visualize the flowing motion from one half pass to another. Think of the perfect flowing balance in the Oriental symbol of yin and yang.

Make sure you position the haunches correctly, meaning not leading, before you start the new half pass. Rhythm is important.

With a young horse, you have to allow three to four steps for the transition between the two half passes. With the trained horse, one straightens for only one stride before flowing into the next half pass.

## THE MENTAL IMAGERY
## OF TURNING THE ARENA WALL

Visualizing the arena wall as a mentally movable object as you ride is a valuable technique, because by using it you can maintain the consistency of the position of the horse more easily.

At the beginning of the training of the horse, one rides the movements in relationship to the wall of the ring. The advantage for the beginning rider is that he visually knows where he is going. The more experienced rider or teacher will use the prin-

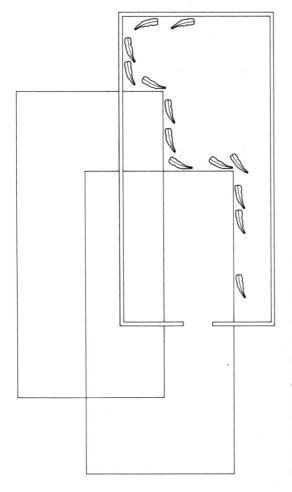

*Two diagrams of the turning of the wall. The simple one shows the visualization of the moving of the walls parallel to each other, going from a shoulder-in to a haunches-in, to establish your bend correctly.*

ciple of mentally turning the wall to maintain the bend of the horse, whatever movement the horse is performing. The advantage for the horse is not having to change his basic position from shoulder-in in the corner to haunches-in out of the corner. He changes the direction in which he moves in this position, but not the position itself, because mentally the rider pretends that it is the wall that has moved.

Afterward, the rider can ride down the center line, keeping the latter as the thrust of his direction while allowing the horse to change position relative to the center line. In other words, the

*The more difficult one shows the turning of the wall where you can visualize any position you want. The same goes for the diagonal, which helps for the half pass.*

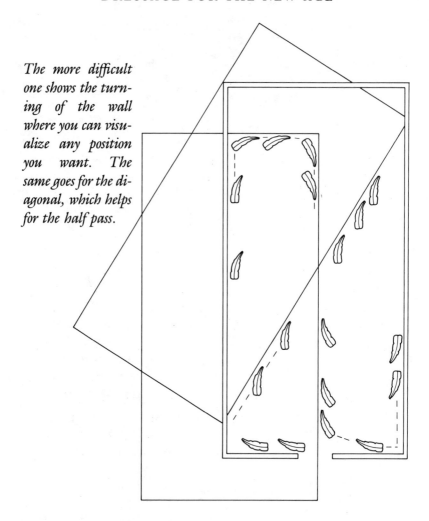

shoulder-in is done on the center line, and then the rider goes into haunches-in, followed by a short diagonal back to the track on the wall. If the bend is lost, one can go back to the shoulder-in on the quarterline.

From shoulder-in to haunches-in, I make my direction the most important thing. For training, I consider bend first and lightness second. Therefore, I adapt the direction in which I want to go to my need for consistency of the bend and for lightness.

Instead of correcting the balance of the horse, I ask him for the same movement in a different direction. (See the figures on pages 143 and 144.) For example, if the horse is in shoulder-in and progressively loses impulsion in collection, I will ask him to go into a small circle in shoulder-in, which requires more impulsion in collection. That way he has to rebalance himself to give me that movement in a different direction. This is psychologically valuable because I did not correct him. I made him aware of his own mistake and pointed out to him that he has to put himself in a different position to give me the movement that I asked for. He himself knows how he has to be balanced in order to perform that movement. That is education.

# 19

# The Countercanter, Flying Change, and Tempi Changes

## COUNTERCANTER

The countercanter is very important for improving the general balance of the gait. It should be done as soon as the rider feels it is possible (even though it may be somewhat acrobatic) and as soon as the true canter is reasonably balanced.

In the training of the horse, one uses the countercanter to work on the straightness of the horse, using the movement to obtain the quality canter. (One uses both the true canter and the countercanter to train the rider not to lean forward, and to have a loose leg with no tension in it.)

The countercanter is the same thing as the true canter, except that it is ridden more carefully. You must have a stronger visualization, paying extra attention to the projection of the mind as well as to the position and relaxation of the body of the rider.

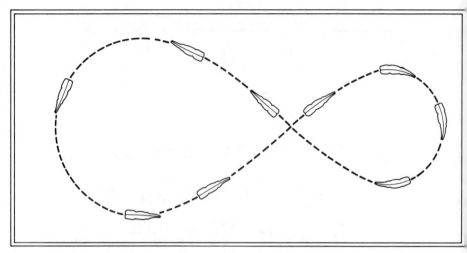

*Countercanter: Making a small loop for true canter and a larger one for the countercanter.*

Here again, as for the half pass, one can use the "moving of the walls" technique, mentally moving and placing the arena wall on the side opposite the horse's leading leg. You then use your imagination: Pretend you are cantering to the right when you want to countercanter to the left.

One looks for balance, rhythm, and relaxation from the horse in the countercanter. At the beginning, the head position is not very important. Allow the horse's head to be the way he wants it to be and you will correct it later on.

Always remember that the countercanter is just a change of direction to either the left or the right. Nothing changes as far as the rider's position goes. The rider has to keep the same position as for the normal canter; his outside shoulder is back and his outside leg (outside in relation to the bend) is back. The rider looks in the direction in which he wants to go. If the rider gives direction with his hands, it will upset the horse by pulling his head to the inside and he will switch leads. Once again, it is very important to keep the same rhythm. Keep the impulsion by re-inforcing your outside leg, keeping a light contact with it, whether the horse is straight or slightly bent.

Be sure you give yourself the mental space to do the countercanter by keeping away from the walls. Visualize the entire circle as you countercanter. When I teach people to do the countercanter, I try to make it easy for them. First the rider canters on a large, round loop along the long side (see the figure on page 148), then on a small circle in true canter. Then he goes off on the diagonal and does his circle in countercanter, returning on the next diagonal to true canter. In other words, he does a figure 8.

Another mental help: When you do the first half of the circle, which is a small one in true canter, followed by a bigger one in your countercanter, give yourself and your horse lots of mental space: Don't go all the way to the wall because it may cause the horse to panic and switch leads.

I say to never get close to the walls in the countercanter circle. When it's done on a large circle away from the wall, the horse can do it easily because he has all this enormous mental space in which to work.

If there is a problem with countercanter, then the rider must check to see if he is using his hands too much to get his direction. If the rider stiffens his hands, legs, or feet too much, if there is too much pushing, a lack of respect for rhythm (which causes a lack of balance), a lack of mental planning or projection, or the horse is not ready or supple enough to perform the movement, then one has to go back to these basics.


## THE FLYING CHANGE

In nature, the horse changes his canter lead because he changes direction. Changing the canter lead while going in the same direction is a complication devised by man's mind. Nevertheless, there is the horse that does the flying changes and the horse that learns the flying changes. There is also the horse that likes the flying changes and the horse that doesn't like them. Some horses show off with them. For others, the changes are too hard.

There's a lot of controversy about horses with long backs and horses with short backs being more or less able to do the changes. I think that back length has little to do with it. What is important is a quality canter on both reins.

Flying change can be easy when you have a quality canter in the correct rhythm and a horse that is straight, and the horse has learned to do a correct countercanter, and the canter-to-walk transition.

The most important thing in going into flying change is to see the movement first in your mind, so that you take an attitude that is both mental as well as physical. You are telling your horse, "I am in this position for you to give me the movement I visualize." Visualization plus body position allows the movement to happen.

Actually, the rider unconsciously rides this way all the time, if he is not riding totally physically. The position of the rider for the canter depart is the same as for the half pass. It is mental visualization that decides which movement you are going to do. That's why you have to keep your images very clear. Even if you do use exactly the same physical position, what is important is the *mental meaning* behind it.

For the flying change, you need to have a very round canter. The horse can't be flat. One has to look at the flying change as a new strike-off at the canter, because that is what it is, with the horse round and going "up." It is during the suspension, when his legs are up in the air, that he has to switch. If he is flat, it is not possible for him to change correctly.

If your horse is relaxed, you should ask him, by putting the hands higher, to be a little more straight, channeled, or nearly rigid, with his back a little more up under you. As soon as the horse feels that, he is going to know that is the position that leads to the flying change.

I never talk about timing. The way I teach it, first you have to put the horse in the position of the new canter lead. Only after you have the position do you ask for the flying change.

First the rider positions his body, with both hands a little higher than normal (how much higher depends on the conformation of the horse), with a little more contact on both reins in order to have the spine of the horse rise *up* underneath the rider.

That way the horse can do the flying change, front and back legs at the same time.

Then the rhythm and the timing are given with the use of the rider's outside leg three times, followed by the inside leg. That is to say, to help the visualization, while on the left rein I use my outside or right leg in rhythm with the canter every stride for three strides. Before the fourth stride I ask for the flying change by using the *new outside* or left leg a little back. The horse has to be *very straight* when I do this.

The timing of the new outside hand, which occurs just before the new outside leg goes on, is like two electric shocks very close to each other. The new inside rein, which is the right rein, must be loose so the horse's shoulder can change and come forward with the new leading leg.

Some horses will change if touched with just the rider's leg, and some horses will change with just a pressure of the finger on the new outside rein. At the very beginning, there has to be a sharp electric touch with the new outside leg, and later you refine it to nearly nothing. There must be no tension in the rider's thighs or knees. If your leg is contracted, you won't be able to give that little electric touch to change things.

That's why at the countercanter the rider's leg already has to be relaxed and loose, with no tension in the knee and thigh. If the rider's leg is tense, then the horse is tense and doesn't feel the rider's leg. The same problem will occur if there is too much contact with the hand.

When I teach the canter and the countercanter I keep in mind the flying change. Failing to master these is the reason why one often has such a hard time afterward with the flying change.

The flying change is best done from the countercanter just after the corner. That reinforces the power of the new outside rein. An easier thing for the horse, because of the attraction of the wall, but harder for the rider, is to do the flying change from true canter to countercanter right after the corner at the beginning of the long side. (Just after the corner is a magic spot.) Then the horse is in countercanter against the wall and he is straight.

As soon as you get the flying change on both leads, do them

wherever you want to. If you don't get them, stop and redo them, but as soon as you get two good changes on both sides, quit. Give the horse lots of praise when he's done the change. Do not *work* on flying changes; do not do twenty or thirty of them. Do one or two on each rein and then forget them for a week. Don't make a big deal of them. Keep it low key.

Generally the flying change on one side is going to be easier than on the other. The side that is difficult will be 90 percent due to lack of quality of the canter. That's why I like to begin in the order of training with the pirouette first, before the flying changes, because most of the time it will improve the quality of the canter.

Let me now address a few of the difficulties you may encounter with this movement. The major problem in doing flying change is in keeping the horse straight. Be sure you are sitting balanced and square in the saddle.

If you have trouble visualizing the flying change, try this physical exercise, which will make visualization more precise: Do six strides of canter and then flying change, six strides of canter and halt. If the horse kicks out at the moment you ask for flying change, it is because you are doing too much.

What about the horse that loses suspension after flying change work is introduced and the canter becomes four-beat? Generally a horse that is collected too soon gets shorter and flatter in the canter. He gets shrunken. You have to go back to a rolling canter. Perhaps your canter becomes flat and you lose impulsion, but the four-beat canter is very rare. Most of the time the four-beat canter does not exist. It takes a lot of work to produce it.

It could be that something is being done by the rider so strongly that it affects the horse's gait—too much use of the hands, perhaps. The thinking is wrong there. The rider wants to shorten the canter by using force. Again, you have to return to a good, rolling, too-much-forward canter. Think of the extended canter, then work on haunches-in at the canter, and make sure the inside rein is, in fact, loose. At the same time, think about collection coming from the rider's position and not from the rider's compression of the horse. Don't compress; that is a misunderstanding of collection. As soon as you lose the quality of your canter, stop and try it again. Too much cantering can also cause the quality of the gait to be lost. When you canter, do it for a short time.

What if the horse's brains become fried about the single flying change and he comes off the bit and speeds up his rhythm in anticipation at $X$ or wherever it is the change occurs? This situation can indicate too much work on flying changes and ignoring the quality of the canter itself, as well as not paying enough attention to relaxation in the movement.

The rider must go back to square one. Don't do flying changes. Go back to the quality of the canter and complete relaxation of the horse and rider. Eliminate anticipation by the rider using the "two minds" technique. The front part of the mind says, "No, I'm not going to do flying changes anymore, I am only going to work on a quality canter." Then, when everything is right and perfect, the back part of the mind says, "Yes, I'm going to do a flying change right here."

## TEMPI CHANGES

People make a big deal out of tempi changes. They need to give themselves more mental space, and relax about them. Tempi changes are just a succession of one flying change after another.

To do them, you have to learn how to visualize and how to count, because if the horse can do a flying change on either leg, there's no problem with doing them in sequence if the balance and the rhythm stay the same.

I usually start by doing changes every two strides ("the twos") instead of every three or four, because there's a magic rhythm to the twos. But stay aware and keep it from becoming a routine where the horse gets to be an automaton. The horse can get so into the rhythm that he counts for the rider.

Start with three changes every two strides, followed by five, then seven. Do not spend fifteen days concentrating on nothing but the twos, because you will lose your single change; again, the horse will start to get mechanized.

When you have mastered the twos, go to changes every four strides, then every three strides. Then go back and forth among the different numbers. Overdoing it, however, will also lead to mechanization on the part of the horse. I would recommend doing only two or three series of tempi changes at a time. It is something to check out, but don't "work" on them if they are there.

Do the tempi changes calmly, visualizing them as a single flying change done after another single flying change. It is just a matter of counting. In the beginning you need a lot of visualization. After the horse knows what is expected of him, do as little physically as you can.

If you get in trouble, stop and redo it as calmly as you can, always checking to see if the problem is with straightness or with rhythm. If so, go back to the quality of the canter, making sure the horse is light and round, and on the outside rein, and in a good balance. Or perhaps it is a question of your doing too much; in that case go back to lightness and noninterference.

If during tempi changes across the diagonal the horse charges for the wall after the second change and becomes too strong, once again it is because there is too much compression, too much contact, too much action for the flying change. The horse is getting more and more upset. Go back to the quality of the canter and try to do much less in asking for the flying change.

The flying change every stride is not a canter. It is a jumping gait, since the horse jumps from lateral to lateral (pair of legs) to accomplish it. One of the hardest things to do is to give the horse the idea of the timing you want in the flying change every stride, because it happens very fast. At the beginning you do three changes every stride, starting with the side with the easy change, followed by the "hard" side, and then the "easy" change again. As soon as the horse understands that, add two more. Go from three to five, and from five to seven.

Flying change every stride is a difficult movement to teach to others; in fact, very few people know how to teach it. The timing involved is so fast that people get confused. They need to have a calm mind and, at the same time, very fast timing, and this is what is so difficult to get across in teaching it.

That is why I say it is necessary to do less in the beginning of the training of the horse and rider. One must work smarter, not harder, looking forward to the day when you will do flying change every stride. As soon as the rider is moving his seat bones, he is interfering; any leaning forward, any shifting with the weight, gripping with the thighs, doing anything too much, will disturb the horse. Always do less and you will see the horse is going to pick up your thinking faster than he will from your seat bones. Try to remove as much physical interference as you can in your riding.

# 20

# *Piaffer/Passage*

There is no rule that dictates which movement, *piaffer* or *passage,* comes first. You need a great deal of knowledge and experience before you know which one to start first with each particular horse. If there is a rule, it is that if one comes more naturally to the horse, try to work on the other one first.

Other times, however, you should develop the one that is more natural first, hoping to help the one that is not. Sometimes, teaching the *passage* first will give a better diagonalization and rhythm in the *piaffer*. Sometimes learning the *piaffer* will help the horse prepare for a better collected trot.

Normally, however, when I start the horse in *piaffer*, it is, as I say, because the *passage* is very natural, and going into the

Piaffer: *Irish Hill* (PHOTO: KATHY CLEAVER).

*piaffer* for him is harder. It is more rare that I start with the *passage*; I generally start with the *piaffer*.

At times I do a lot of rein back as a preparation for both the *piaffer* and the *passage,* depending on the case, in order to make the horse rounder. The rein back is similar to the *piaffer* in that both are diagonal gaits, so sometimes the former helps the diagonalization of the latter.

The creation of impulsion *before* and not during the movements, especially at the beginning of the movements, is very important for *piaffer* and *passage,* much more so than for the other movements.

At the beginning, what you are looking for is two to four strides maximum of *piaffer* and *passage;* you are looking for the regularity of stride and the correct diagonalization. Do not go for elevation too soon—that's deadly. You need to get the soft *pas-*

*sage* and the low *piaffer* first, and with as much mental approach and as little physical interference as possible. You set up your own trap for failure when you do it physically. The *mental freshness* of the horse is the most important element in both.

The hand position is very important for general balancing and lightness of the horse. You have to determine where to put the head, and where the height of the front end should be in relation to the rear end. It is a very fragile balancing. The less you interfere with that balance, the better. Sometimes you use a slight balancing movement of the hands sideways for helping the diagonalization of the *piaffer*. If it is done very slightly, it should not cause the horse to rock. (If done in the *passage*, it can cause a roll in the movement.)

I generally do the *piaffer* on the snaffle only, and most of the time from the walk. You can also do it from slowing down the collected trot, from the halt, or from the rein back. When the horse can stop without the rein, he is ready for *piaffer*. The *piaffer* is to allow the horse to be round; he must be absolutely on the bit. I use the *piaffer* to teach straightness and roundness, not as a goal in itself.

Most of the time I use the *piaffer* to straighten the horse. It gives you a lot of indication where the horse is crooked and why. He tells you in what position he is able to *piaffer*. If it is too unorthodox, try to make it a little better and smoother afterward, but that's the position you are going to have to put him in to begin the *piaffer*. What is important is the spirit in which you do the movement, not the movement itself.

In the *piaffer*, always keep the horse fresh in his mind. If the horse is able to give you six strides, ask him for five and no more. You should never go beyond his willingness and ability.

*Piaffer* is hard for most riders, but it is easy for me. I believe it is because I think that the essence of the movement is lightness. Because I work my horses in lightness so much of the time, *piaffer* is easy for them to do. On the other hand, one of the hardest things for me to do is to create *passage* in relaxation without taking advantage of resistance.

Most riders feel *passage* is easy because they do it in resis-

Passage: *Dom Giovanni, Sun Valley* (PHOTO: MARCIA HART).

tance. (*Passage* can take more abuse and compromise than *piaffer*.) The horse is blocked on one side of the mouth and they compress him into resistance.

It is very difficult to create a *passage* in relaxation; one needs a lot of visualization and the feeling of upward movement. To achieve this, the rider cannot block in front with the hands, since he has to make space for the horse to go up, to elevate.

In doing the *piaffer* from the walk, the *piaffer* is in that walk, that is, the walk must contain the *piaffer*. Think about trot on the spot, use maybe a click of the tongue, think the rhythm, tap-tap with the whip. Try this before the horse begins the movement, not during. You tap the top of the croup for *piaffer*, from the saddle, because if you touch him on the side, you may have a lateral movement of the croup.

The *piaffer* is the essence of collection. The horse is *plein de feu*, full of fire, and doesn't go anywhere. It has to be done in

Passage *on the long reins: Aliendro, Morgan stallion, Sun Valley* (*PHOTO: KATHY CLEAVER*).

*complete* lightness; when you compress the horse, everything stops.

Sometimes too much collection works against the horse. When the horse gets too close to the *levade,* he gets stuck. You have to open him up, create less engagement of the hindquarters (not a common problem).

The rider's body for the *piaffer* is also in a position of extreme collection; the legs are back, the shoulders back with the chest up toward the sky, the head up. Always remember, you must still have a loose back to go with the movement of the horse. The hands are generally a little higher than normal and very quiet, with as little movement as possible. The rider's legs have to be loose.

Some horses have more height of leg in this movement. If you have too much movement in front, lower your hands; if you do not have enough action in front, elevate your hands, which lowers the haunches and makes the front even with the back.

Levade: *Jabute, trained by Mestre Nuno Oliveira, Quinta do Brejo* (*PHOTO: FRANCINE HALKINS*).

I repeat, you must create fantastic impulsion before you start. Always try to create impulsion before the movement and not during, because balance in these movements is very fragile, and if you interfere you are going to cause trouble.

Creating impulsion with visualization is important for the *piaffer*, because you can't make the horse do the *piaffer* physically. You cannot afford to use your leg. Think impulsion, forward, straight, and going nowhere on the spot, with very little stepping forward at the beginning, just an inch at a time. Try doing *piaffer* and *passage* outdoors, where you have a lot more natural impulsion. Use the horse's natural excitement to start.

The biggest problem riders have is that the horse is not in a position where he can perform, and the rider forces him to do it with the leg and the hand. The horse has to find the position in

Levade *on the long reins: Aliendro, Sun Valley* (PHOTO: KATHY
CLEAVER).

which he can do it by himself; you cannot force him. It is hard
enough for him to do it if he's in his best position. That's why
you often see the horse do three steps and then collapse. Spurs
generally don't help either. They contract the horse; the rider
gets stuck and is contracted as well. When you use your legs, you
contract the horse's body and then you need to pick the horse up
with your hands—and that's worse. Once again, the less you do
with your legs, the better off you are, or you do the *piaffer* in
resistance.

With the *passage*, sometimes it is helpful to use the beginning of the Spanish walk as a help. That gives you the elevation
in the front. Sometimes one teaches the Spanish walk before
*passage*, but rarely, only as a last resort.

To *passage*, if the horse does not happen to have the *piaffer*
first, you generally start from the school trot, which leads to the
*doux passage* or soft *passage*. The school trot is a sophisticated
collected trot, with the maximum of collection you can have in a
trot. Look for the quality school trot, then slow it down and go
into the *doux passage*, where you work on the regularity of the

diagonalization before going for more elevation by bringing your shoulders back. Sometimes using a light alternating leg, right and left, helps the rider get more diagonalization and elevation in the *passage*.

As soon as you get the thought of the *passage* in the horse's head, and he begins to do it, stop. Use good judgment and don't spend too much time working on it; nor should you have to work on the *passage* for three years until you get it.

Look for a *passage* as round as possible with maximum engagement of the hindquarters, depending on conformation. The quality of the *passage* is in the length of time of suspension, what we call *tride* in French. Again, the less interference from the rider, the better.

What if the horse has the soft *passage,* but refuses to put real power into it for the real thing? If the horse is active for the school trot, and if he is very light, he will have the same activity for the *doux passage*. If there is too much contact with the hand and too much compression with the leg, the more you ask for collection, the less you will get it. You do not grab the horse with the hand and push him with the leg, because you kill the *passage* that way.

This is the moment of truth. The horse has to go *up*. Go back to lightness and give more room to the horse's back to go up under you. You need a very light, feeling lower back for this.

When both the *piaffer* and *passage* are established, try for the transition from one to the other. This has to be done mentally as much as possible, because anything physical is going to destroy the rhythm. The rider's back is straighter for the *piaffer,* and you have to go *with* but *up* at the same time. Out of the *piaffer,* you allow the *passage* by loosening the back and allowing a little more forward movement. The rider's back is still up but more forward, more round to allow the forward motion.

Try to make the upper part of the rider's back a little straighter to go back to the *piaffer* from the *passage*. Basically, the rider follows the nature of the movement and the back of the horse.

Some horses have more ability than others. Some horses

have ability in one movement and difficulty in the other. It is rare to find a good transition between one and the other. Transitions will be good if your horse has a *piaffer* that is round and collected, not one in which he is "sitting on the haunches" too much.

Nobody knows how to do *piaffer* and *passage* well with their horses today because they try to do too much. The horses do them because the riders make them do them. It is unpleasant to see a horse forced to do them, but *piaffer* and *passage* are the most artistically fulfilling movements when correctly done and the horse participates willingly.

# 21

## Spanish Walk
## and Trot

Even though they are not recognized as official movements in dressage, the Spanish gaits are, first of all, very aesthetic ones. The Spanish trot, for example, is one of the most spectacular and thrilling movements, resembling a *passage* with an extended fore-leg. Second, they can be very beneficial for the horse, especially in loosening up a limited action of the shoulder. They can also help the rider develop tact, timing, and the ability to think quickly while in motion in the saddle.

The Spanish gaits are a learning process where the rider, from the ground, artificially teaches the horse to lift as high as possible, first one and then the other front leg—*la jambette,* very much like a French cancan, as my grandfather called it.

These movements require a very experienced rider. They

should not be abused, as a Spanish gait generally works against collection and leads to a hollow back.

Begin at the halt, from the ground. Begin tapping with the whip, using a light touch, on the horse's leg at different levels, until he reacts. When he lifts his leg, or strikes, reward him with a treat.

Once he understands this well, begin the one-step, while still on the ground, walking alongside the horse. Touching him with the whip, with one hand on the rein, the lifting of the leg is obtained on one side at the walk. Be sure that the horse is really straight, and his head carriage high. Then reverse and do the same thing on the opposite side. Then, sit on the horse and repeat the technique. As soon as you begin work on the Spanish walk from the saddle, you will carry two whips, one in each hand.

You obtain *la jambette* by tapping with the whip from the saddle, with the rein corresponding to the leg that is to be lifted held slightly higher. Once again, you obtain the lifting of the leg at the halt first, and then at the walk.

In the Spanish walk, one must remember that the *walk* is very important. Sometimes we get very involved in that *jambette* feeling. Obtain the walk as soon as possible, as the horse can easily get stuck at the halt.

Use your outside leg, your leg opposite *la jambette,* to go forward. It is on just as a light pressure. Start the Spanish walk with just the lifting of the left leg of the horse, always expecting the walk. Do one step asking for nothing, then ask for the lifting of the left leg in Spanish walk every step.

After that, you are going to reverse and do the same thing on the opposite, or right, leg. Next, you are going to do the three-step: *jambette* left, *jambette* right, *jambette* left. Then walk normally. Then *jambette* again for three strides.

You have both hands higher, to elevate the forehand, and one hand a little higher on the side where you want to produce *la jambette.* As soon as you feel the horse's left shoulder going up, use your right leg to ask him to go forward, nearly at the same time. In order for this timing to occur, the rider has to be thinking ahead. The sequence is the rein (a light closing of the fingers) and then the rider's leg. Then, as the right shoulder comes up, the rider's left leg asks the horse to go forward.

Always start with the "easy" leg first, followed by the "hard" one, then the easy one. Make sure that your own leg stays loose. That way you don't produce excitement. Too much tightness, too much tenseness, too much compression will upset the horse.

The rider must make sure he has a quiet attitude that keeps his body movement to a minimum, because the movement, done correctly, has a roll to it. The rider has to stay straight, in a normal walk position, and try to avoid rolling. Also, the rider should not lean on the horse's forehand, which some inadvertently do by looking down to watch the leg come up.

The three-step helps to keep the walk going, and you can return to it whenever you want for that purpose. Basically you work for a long period of time on the three-step in order to make this movement clear and easy for the horse.

The Spanish trot is similar to the walk, except that it feels like a *passage* with an extension of the front leg. You combine the two movements, using the two whips to get the extension.

These are two movements with which horse and rider can have a lot of fun.

---

# 22

---

# *Canter on the Spot and Canter Backward*

For both these movements, the rider needs the extreme quality of a perfect three-beat canter without any resistance or contraction. The horse must be highly supple and flexible and have the ability to collect himself into that perfect three-beat canter. It is very important for the rider not to interfere with the basic mechanism of the canter. He must follow and "listen" to the movement of the horse's back in order to be "with" him and not to overdo.

For example, in doing the canter pirouette the rider must think about where he wants to go, which is toward the inside and toward the back instead of a completely forward motion. That is what the rider wants to exaggerate instead of the forward movement.

For the canter on the spot, the rider has to equalize the forward and backward motion. It is done by reducing the canter. The forward movement of the canter is slowed until one is cantering on the spot. However, once again, the most important thing is the quality of the gait. If the rider grabs the horse with his hands, the movement will stop; instead the rider should retard the movement with his shoulders. In other words, the rider should increase collection.

This movement is very similar in feeling to the pirouette, but the rider doesn't actually go into the pirouette; be aware, however, that it is much easier to reduce the canter in haunches-in (which is the basic position of the pirouette) than when the horse is straight in the canter.

The regular canter is an ellipselike movement in which the movement of the saddle goes from the back to the front and from the outside to the inside.

Therefore, the most important part of doing the canter backward is to be aware when one is actually going backward in the gait, and allow this motion to become bigger. Very few horses are able to perform this movement.

# AFTERWORD

Like other students of dressage who have experienced the harmony between horse and rider that, once achieved, is a kind of rapture, I have been willing to pursue every and any means of making this elusive connection mine once again, at will, with other horses. I have cried tears, bruised and torn my body, forfeited my cash, traveled afar, read every line written on the subject, listened to anyone who would talk about it, and even exploited my profession as a journalist to relentlessly ask questions of those who seemed to know. I have learned it is not something one can do mechanically, or by force, and still call beautiful. Something else has to be involved. I have known Dominique Barbier for more than a dozen years. I have ridden horses he has trained and especially enjoyed their exceptional ease in performing the *piaffer* in lightness. I have applied, with success, what he has taught me about the mental side of riding. I believe that what he teaches is the closest one can come to expressing in words what the unique feeling of dancing with one's horse is like and how one best prepares oneself to achieve this state of grace. Through this book I hope you can be helped to have this experience of beauty, through developing a better relationship with your horse and its willing partnership in the dance of centaurs.

—MARY DANIELS

# INDEX

174